# The Angel Came

## Dr. Ophelia G. Griggs

ISBN 978-1-0980-0569-6 (paperback)
ISBN 978-1-0980-0570-2 (digital)

Christian Faith Publishing, Inc.
832 Park Avenue
Meadville, PA 16335
www.christianfaithpublishing.com

Printed in the United States of America

# *Dedication*

In memory of my beloved mother, Lula Mae "Peggy" Griggs Moyer; brother, Spencer O'Neil Moyer; and maternal grandfather, George Washington Griggs.

For my family, the Griggs and Geter family, and childhood friend, Mary Lisa Williamson, who passed last April 21, 2018, love you, Auntie!

# Canonical Note

He hath made everything beautiful in his time:
also he hath set the world in their heart,
so that no man can find out the work that God
maketh from the beginning to the end.

—Ecclesiastes 3:11 (KJV)

# Contents

# Author's Note

The events in the book are authentic and experienced by the author. I view the events as supernatural treasures that are beyond human comprehension but mysterious enough to realize and accept that there is another life afar from the earthly realm.

The book specifies supernatural occurrences that are not to evoke fright but are my shared experiences that reveal awareness about divine encounters that, most likely, many can attest but possibly are hesitant to disclose. My purpose is to incite the silent voices to voice their similar stories to others too. Some of the episodes in the narrative will not include names or indicate glorious event details to protect identity. It is possible that some of the recollections regarding my brother whom my mother birthed could be slightly *hit* or *miss* memories.

# *Acknowledgments*

First it is essential that I acknowledge my Lord and Savior Jesus Christ. The Lord has been my guide through the entire writing of this book. It is because of him that I have been able to write the two most difficult chapters which pertain to my brother and mother.

I would like to thank Veronica R. Dancy whom I consider as a spiritual mother in Christ for believing in me through her outward show of enthusiasm and encouragement.

I would like to express thanks to others (you know who you are) who said with a smile, "I look forward to reading your book, or I can't wait to read your book."

Your statement added a push to me completing the book. It held me accountable to follow through.

Last but not the least, thanks with a big smile to a few coworkers who assisted me without hesitation to conquer a couple Microsoft Word 2016 challenges. Thanks to the reference desk librarians at Martinsville Public Library and at the Collinsville Public Library location.

# Review: King James Version

Peaking the author's interest about the King James Bible origin because of its grammar and punctuation usage, the origination writings were in Hebrew (Old Testament), Aramaic, and Greek (New Testament), and later, several translations emerged such as Latin. However, the initial KJV, also known as the King James Bible, is an authorized English translation Bible used by the Christian Church of England. This Bible had its beginning in 1604 and its completion in 1611. Since the KJV of the Bible has been around for years, as early as the 7th century, it is *public domain* (can be used liberally without constraint and prior consent).

With the above indication, every biblical scriptures in this book cited by the author are solely from the KJV of the Bible. Some of the scriptures will indicate KJV after it and some do not give the translation. Nevertheless, the scriptures without translation are not from other biblical versions, and if so, the author would indicate it.

The author purposely used the KJV for scriptural sources. As a result, readers could enrich their Bible study skills, as well as seek out several translations from other biblical interpretations of his or her choosing to parallel numerous versions at the same time.

## *Source*

Bibleinfo.com.(2012).What is the history of the King James Bible? Retrieved from http://www.bibleinfo.com/en/questions/history-kjv

Wikipedia. (2018, March 15). King James Version. [The free encyclopedia]. Retrieved from https://en.wikipedia.org/wiki/King_James_Version

# CHAPTER 1

## *Cut at the Soul*

My brother Spencer was the result from a marriage that did not work out for my mother. I always viewed him as my whole brother because we came from the same womb, just had different fathers. He latched onto me like Jacob who took ahold of his twin brother Esau's heel when he came out the womb (Genesis 25:26). There were many times that I sneaked out the house because if he saw me leaving, he would cry big teardrops, calling a portion of my name *Pheia* while extending his arms toward me saying, "I wanna go."

Spencer was born when I was a student in the sixth grade at Figsboro Elementary School, and how well I remember the news about my mother birthed him. Presently Figsboro Elementary is no longer operating as an elementary school. The school building is not closed. It is used for educational programs and has always been a voting precinct location. When the news came to me, I was outside the classroom.

Still to this day, I cannot remember if my teacher shared the news or the secretary from the office. All I know is that I had to go outside of the classroom (hmm, maybe I did go to the office), and the news of my brother's birth struck every emotion inside me. The news caused tears to well up in my eyes. At the time, I did not know if the tears occurred because I did not want a brother (no sibling ever). I wanted to stay as the only child, or maybe the tears were for an unfortunate situation that later on led to the death of my brother.

Additionally, my brother was premature, and his picture was in the local newspaper. A nurse at Memorial Hospital of Martinsville and Henry County (now known as SOVAH Health of Martinsville) favored him and provided care to him until he met medical approval to come home. He was a preemie baby. Spencer was so small lying on a pillow that it encased him like a glove on a person's hand. Amazed by what I saw, I would say, "The pillow swallows him up!" He was a cute chocolate drop with smooth black hair. Our maternal aunt favored him too. People used to state to our mother, "You had Spencer and Ophelia for your sister."

The birth of my brother taught me about caring for a child, and a bond grew between us. My mother would wash his cloth diapers and hang them on the clothesline in the backyard that somewhat slopes down the hill. When the cloth diapers dried, I would get them off the clothesline, but guess what? The clothesline remained in the backyard, and the occasional use is a bird or two flying to it. Usually when I am washing dishes and looking out the kitchen window, I see a bird or two on the clothesline. I watched them fly back and forth as if they were playing a game.

When I was sixteen years old and school out for the summer break, I would feed my brother and take him to his doctor's appointments for his *baby shots*. My mother worked in one of the local furniture factories that is nonexistent today as a place of employment for the community. Actually, the major industries that Martinsville and Henry County known for have left the area. Anyhow, when my brother and I waited for him to be seen by the doctor, I had thoughts like, "I wonder if they (mothers there with their child) think I am my brother's mother?" My brother cried when he saw the needle, and I squeezed my toes. He cried big teardrops and stretched toward me to save him from the immunization shots, but I knew he had to get those shots. Therefore, I held him and said comforting words that let him know I will not let anything happen to him.

I'm amused while reminiscing a time when I loved to eat my brother's Gerber apricots and one time drinking a few sips of his apple juice right from his bottle. He looked at me with his beautiful brown eyes, and those eyes expanded wider when he laughed at seeing his sister drink from his bottle. It tickled him so, and from that point on, he would extend his bottle that contained milk toward me as if I would drink it. Little did he know I was not about to drink his milk. I did not like milk and still do not like it. I am lactose intolerant!

Furthermore, I recall the joys of seeing my brother learn how to walk. He got his behind pinched when he stood to walk and immediately tried to sit. His little butt got pinched before he would do an actual sit, and he thought that was funny too. He was a late walker, not walking at the age he should as indicated for any child during their development. He was well near one and a half years old, but he was talking good! I remember our mother taking him for rides in her car, an old model light blue four-door Ford Falcon (cannot remember year of car) to get him to sleep. Sometimes we (my mother, aunt, and I) took turns rocking Spencer to sleep. Whenever one of us laid him on the bed to sleep, he would bang his head on the pillow. Eventually, he grew out of banging his head. Thank God for that!

Moreover, as I am ruminating about my brother, I am experiencing an overwhelming feeling that makes me say *wow!* There are numerous memorable stories I could share about him. One memory about Spencer refers to our aunt who is an awesome licensed barber! I am smiling as I reflect on our aunt using Spencer to practice the latest haircut styles. The haircuts that stood out the most on him were the military look and initials carved into the haircut. He always had a fresh haircut that displayed our aunt's talent. She taught my brother and me how to drive an automatic and a 4-and-5-speed-stick shift car. When Spencer got his driver's license, he drove our aunt to Greensboro, North Carolina, most times on Fridays when she got off work. Of course, sometimes, he would stay the weekend. He knew how to get around in the Greensboro area better than I could.

A second memory is when Spencer was five, he loved for him and me to play Cynthia and Tyrone. Whenever I was cleaning the bathroom, putting on makeup, or combing my hair, he would say, "Let's play Cynthia and Tyrone." Then he would sit on the commode facing the commode handle. The commode, in his imaginary mind, was his motorcycle and the plunger, well, was the gear stick.

Motorcycle with a gear stick? What? Funny! He would call me Cynthia and if I forget and say "What do you want, Spencer?" he'd say, "Call me Tyrone."

If I say *Tyrone*, he'd say *Cynthia*. Then we laugh, and he would shift gears using the plunger while making a drum, drum sound. *Cynthia* and *Tyrone* were his childhood imaginary names for us.

One day, out of the blue, he told me that I was *Cynthia* and he was *Tyrone* when we were both in the bathroom. I was putting on makeup that day, and that is how the *Cynthia-and-Tyrone* make-believe started. He finally stopped the Cynthia-and-Tyrone fantasy at age six.

Another remembrance is Spencer thought he was *Superman*. I am tickled while thinking about this. It is as if it happened yesterday. My aunt purchased him the superhero costume *Superman* for his Halloween character that was his choice. How well do I remember the red plastic cape! Spencer attempted to jump off the back porch several times. One day with his red cape on, he went over to the neighbor's house and thought he would climb the neighbor's big tall tree and jump. The neighbor whom we viewed as a grandmother (deceased) told our mother about her catching Spencer trying to climb her tree to jump, thinking he could fly. Momma took his red cape and threw it away. There were several conversations about *Superman* being not a real person. Bless his heart; he was only six years old thinking he could do what Clark Kent did—fly in the air. Too hilarious!

Lastly a remembrance about Spencer is me leaving home to attend undergraduate school at Norfolk State University, and when I came home during breaks, he would say words that I knew he was not learning in school. He was in elementary school and was nine years old!

My mother would say, "He has been studying the dictionary." Spencer was eager to share the words he learned. He would say the words in correct content and smile his beautiful teeth at me when stating the words appropriately in a sentence. I would smile back at him and feel proud. I would praise him about using astute words. He would say something smart like "You are not the only one learning big words" with a sly grin. And we laughed.

While residing in the Norfolk, Virginia, area after graduating from Norfolk State University, I remember not getting it passed my mind that my brother was not ten years old anymore. Of course, he had grown past the age ten. Nevertheless, when he was in elementary school, I had an unpleasant dream that he died. And on my mother's front door in her house, there was a beautiful white wreath hanging, which was made from plastic trash bags. When I came home for Christmas, lo and behold, the exact Christmas wreath that my brother made in school was hanging on my mother's front door. My brother, I think, was twelve when he made the wreath. I was speechless and never did share that dream with my mother.

I lived in the Tidewater area for about nine years but returned home after yielding to the tugging in my heart, which I knew God was directing me to leave and go back home. I did not want to come back home and had many reasons for wanting to stay in the area. However, I yielded to God's prompting and moved back home.

My aunt helped me move, and I remember becoming sleepy like drifting into a deep sleep while driving. My aunt was in front of me, and she saw me heading toward going off the road. She blew her car horn and flashed her emergency lights. In the split second deep sleep, I could see myself dressed in a white wedding gown walking toward this tall dark brown figure of a man. I could not see his eyes but could see him like a silhouette. My thoughts, in the form of a question, were, *That was death?* I knew I had to return home and that there was a purpose for me to be back home.

Therefore, while being home, the purpose surfaced quickly. My purpose was to assist Momma with rearing my brother. Spencer, without a father figure, knew about God. But he did not have a relationship with God, so he needed salvation. He could cite Psalm 23 and won a trophy when he was middle-school age at a local church where he was baptized the old-fashioned way (in a creek). My brother had aspirations and attempted college at Barber-Scotia. He was interested in the education field. Our aunt gave him everything—from cars to spending money—and doing things for him that a parent would for his or her child. He did not want for anything, and there were *lurkers* in the balance that carried a spirit of jealousy, and my brother could not see it. But I could. My brother was well-known. It was like being with a celebrity whenever we would go to the mall. In addition, later, my mother and I learned that he knew many people not only the ones from Martinsville and Henry County.

My brother graduated from Fieldale-Collinsville High School (FC), but it is now a middle school. I am also a graduate of FC. I graduated in 1981. He played football for the school as well. When he attempted to go to college, he returned home and left the color television there that I gave him. He decided to move out our mother's home, and by then, I had gotten an apartment in the city. Yet before his and my move, he talked about seeing shadows and would see them when I was in a room with him (living room in our mom's house).

I asked him to describe it. And he indicated "It looks like a man," and that would be all that he informed. I was working in the mental health field. I thought maybe he was hallucinating, and I asked, "Are you doing drugs?"

I told him that *people who do cocaine see shadows*. He denied using drugs. My brother and I had long talks about what he was going to do with his life. We talked about Christ, and as typical siblings do, argue sometimes. He always thought he was the oldest, and I was his baby sister. But I was the oldest, and he was my baby brother. However, I got a kick out of it and let him be the big brother.

On one occasion, I recollected my mother, and I rushed to the emergency room because my brother had been badly hurt. He was on a ventilator when we arrived. Of course, my mother was in tears, and I stayed calm. I begin to rub his arm gently and talked to him saying, "Come back to us. Don't leave us."

At one point, I could hear the sound of the machine make a noise, and when I looked at the machine, I saw the blood pressure monitor go down as if it were getting ready to flat line.

I said to my brother, "Don't leave us," several times. And suddenly, I could see the lines that reflected the blood pressure monitoring elevate. I knew that was a good sign. He recovered from that incident and later told me (two months later) about his encounter on the *other side*. He shared it with me first, and I shared it with my mother, our aunt, and anyone that would listen. I recall sharing his story at the second church service (evening service). My brother communicated that he remembered "walking through a tunnel, seeing a bright light at the end of the tunnel, and out of the bright light was a voice saying to him, 'I am not ready for you yet.'"

Spencer became close with my two half-brothers who resulted from my father and his wife union, and he felt I favored them over him. He felt this way only when I treated him with tough love. There were times that his actions warranted tough love. I wanted the best for him and wanted him to be selective in his friend associations. Some of his friends were good for him, so he had a mixture of friends. Spencer had a tight relationship with my two half-brothers. They would hang out and have deep conversations that my brother would disclose to our mother and me. Those conversations have long left me. I could not recall any of those conversations if I tried. The only slight of a conversation I do remember is when Spencer's first cousin was expecting, and he learned her baby's sex (a boy). He was exceedingly overjoyed!

The next excitement from my brother was during summer of 1996 when he called me and said, "You can't guess where I been today, and I went by myself."

My response was, "Where did you go?"

His response, "I went to Richmond, Virginia."

I said, "Richmond. How did you get there?"

He responded, "I rode the bus."

I asked, "What did you go to Richmond for?"

He responded, "I went to take my ASVAB test. I am enlisting in the marines."

My response, "Spencer, I don't know to be happy or cry."

He said, "I met a man too while on the bus, and he was telling me about Jesus Christ. He said the exact same things that you have been telling me."

I smiled with internal joy and said, "Thank you, Jesus!" I could hear the smile in his voice in which I could visually see the smile on his face. I asked, "Was the man a white man or black man?"

His response was, "A white man."

My thoughts went back to a dream I had, and I shared the dream with my brother. I let him know that I dreamed he was on a bus going somewhere. I could see a bright light in the dream, and he was having a conversation with a man, but I did not know the details of the conversation. I further implied that maybe the dream referenced his ride to Richmond and the meeting with the white man who discussed salvation. We discussed when he would leave for basic training and where he was going for the training.

Deep down inside, I was not too at ease about my brother going to the military, but I was glad that he decided to do something constructive with his life since college did not work out for him. I told my brother that he might decide to try college once more when he settles in the military. His response, "Hmm, maybe." I asked him if he had told Momma, and he said, "Not yet."

I said, "Have you told our aunt?"

His response, "Not yet, but I will."

The summer month of 1996, I remember being awakened from my sleep one night and sat straight up in the bed. It was one of those quickened straight-up posture as if seen in the movies (my interpretation of the experience). Immediately, a vision came before me. It was a white casket with my brother in a white suit lying in it. The white color in the vision was bright, pure looking, and I did not become afraid but concerned after the vision was over. I started questioning God. I asked God, "Are you showing me that something is going to happen to my brother while he is in the marines?"

He did not answer me as I was not ready for the answer was my guess. Daily, I prayed. I went on a fast, and the day that I laid prostrate before the Lord in my apartment on the kitchen floor, I could hear him say gently but loudly in my spirit, "Stop praying. Cut it off."

I knew then that my petition went before him, but the outcome would not be as I desired. I can recall wailing and weeping at the altar one Sunday at church. I bent over in agony, but no one knew what I was holding in the depths of my heart, mind, and spirit. I bared a deep burden. In my mind was the thought, *Something was going to happen to my brother while in the marine. And when he leaves for basic training, he would not return alive.* I never did share the vision with my family or my brother. I think later that I shared it with my family, but it was after the thing that I most dreaded took place.

I can ruminate a time while working in the mental health field. I transported a client to Colfax, North Carolina, to get dentures, and the song "I Believe I Can Fly" by singer and songwriter R. Kelly came on the radio. As the client and I listened to the song, I connected the song to my brother but in a spiritual sense and not in a secular sense. I remember telling the client, "I see the song having a spiritual representation in regards to my brother." I told the client, "I do not convey the lyrics of the song as seeing my brother successful in life but see him as wanting to reach something higher not offered in life but heavenward." My client understood and could comprehend spiritual things. This particular client expired in the year of 2016.

In 1996, our mother, who was a great cook and loved to cook, had a compelling drive to prepare Thanksgiving meal for every immediate family member. As I had mentioned earlier, Spencer and I had moved out of the house. He had been out of the house for about three months which, in hindsight, was a preparation for our mom to get accustomed of him not being in the house. The immediate family came to my mother's home to eat Thanksgiving meal. They were my half-brother, the one that is a month younger than my whole brother, our cousins, our aunt, and a few others in the neighborhood shared Thanksgiving meal with us. My brother and half-brother went outside and talked for a long time. I later learned from my mother about the deep conversation between my two brothers.

When Spencer came back in the house, he sat at the table, dressed in a nice white sweat suit that had navy blue stripes down the pant legs and jacket arms. My brother sat in the chair that is in front of the kitchen window. I was standing about half a feet away from him, and our eyes connected. During that moment, I could see the most beautiful aura on him. It appeared as some heavenly glow. I had never seen a glow like that on him before. When someone called either his name or mine, it interrupted us, and the transcendent connection occurring stopped. The thought entered my mind about the vision that I had seen of him *lying in a casket*. I did not entertain the thought too long so I could enjoy family.

However, when I got home that night, I started entertaining the uncanny experience between us. I think my prayer was something like, *Lord, help me help my family to accept what is coming.* I asked God to help me be strong because I knew how close Spencer was to our aunt and to our mom. I remember one day, saying, "Momma, do not make a god out of Spencer."

She did not understand at the time why I would say such a thing. I knew why because of the supernatural occurrences that I encountered and the secret burden that she knew nothing about.

The last month of the year in 1996 approached, and it was the month that Spencer would leave for boot camp. Tuesday, December 17, 1996, supposedly been the day that he reported for basic training at Paris Island. I was at work Friday December 13, 1996. Spencer came by my job. I was in a meeting or having lunch with coworkers. I went to see what my brother wanted (a few dollars), and I could sense a little jealousy. He and I had several conversations about what he wanted to do in life, as well as the same discussion occurred a week before. We talked about life on the phone for three hours. He poured out his heart and repented sorrowfully about many things. I prayed with him and let him know "God forgives you." While praying, I could feel a peace come into my heart when his heart became peaceful.

Well, one of the coworkers told me that I said, "Let me go see what my brother wants because this may be the last time that I see him." I do not remember saying that, and to this day, I still do not remember. Reflecting back on the sense of jealousy, I linked it to my brother that he wanted to do something in life. And the marines may have not been his heart's desire.

Since Tuesday coming up was the schedule date for my brother to leave for basic training, I mentioned to him about coming to church. I told him, "I am speaking at tonight's service."

He mentioned, "I might," but did not show. Before the church service took place, I recollect when it was time to get off work, I felt odd as if something was missing. It was not a good feeling. While I was at church, I felt a heavy burden that words could not describe. I remember sharing the feeling with two of the associate ministers. After the church service, one of the associate ministers whom I had shared how I felt said to me, "After tonight, accept what God allows."

The phone rang between 1:00 a.m. and 2:00 a.m., and it was my mother saying, "Spencer has been shot." She said, "He is at the hospital. Go over to the hospital."

Since I was closer, I went over ahead of her. I called the associate minister who said "After tonight, accept what God allows." The associate minister did not live too far from the hospital, so when I arrived, he was there. I called my mother while driving to the hospital to see if she was on her way and who was bringing her. She said, "Pheia, I feel so tired," and I could hear it in her voice. I knew she was feeling my brother dying.

When I arrived at the hospital and went to the emergency room, the ER doctor came toward me and walked the associate minister and me to a room and said in a saddened voice, "I did all I could do." I screamed with tears rolling down my face. After I had gotten myself together, I told the doctor, "I want to see my brother."

He took me to the room where they tried to revive him. There, my brother laid on the gurney with his eyes opened and lifeless, a fatal shot in the chest. All I could do was look at him with tears coming down my eyes. I walked toward the gurney, looked at him up and down, and saw where his right arm was hanging off the gurney with his hand opened sort of in a downward position.

I told the associate minister, "I want to touch his hand." In my heart, I needed closure. When I touched his hand to hold it, I could feel a warm sensation; and immediately, I experienced a departing from one another. The departing was as if my brother and I held hands, and then he let go.

My mother would later share her phenomenon encounter with my brother prior to his death. She mentioned that Friday while Spencer was in the hall primping in the mirror, she could hear him talking, but it sounded like he was far away. She told me, "I noticed that his eyes looked red, and he denied drinking when I asked. He blew his breath at me to smell that he had not been drinking, and he had not."

She shared he seemed anxious (like he could not be still). She informed a neighbor told me he had been calling all day wanting to know if her grandson had gotten home. He hung out with the neighbor's two grandsons that Friday night going into Saturday morning who witnessed the shooting incident by a *Judas* friend to my brother. I identified the friend as *Judas* because the friend had been to my mother's home and hung out with my brother several times as if the friendship was authentic.

Forgiveness toward *Judas* did not come over night for me. I believe that I have forgiving *Judas* because I am going on with my life not feeling any bitterness in my heart. However, I have not seen *Judas* since the trial. He is out of jail (pulled five years) and cannot come near my family. Truthfully, I do not know if I would remember him if I passed by him on the street unless the Holy Spirit reveals to me that the man I see is him. And knowing me, I would request a few minutes of his time to discuss that *senseless...killing night*.

Momma grieved a long time, but through God's grace and mercy, she coped and reached a point where she could talk about Spencer without crying. She could reflect on him with a smile and share comical things he did or said.

We both had to get grief counseling. I attended the grief group at the local hospital three times. Momma attended one time, but she did seek counseling from the local mental health agency. I recall not needing the group after I was the group facilitator for the third meeting. Preparing my presentation was a healing process that begun for me. In addition, grief counseling was not new for me because being employed at the local mental health agency and discussing grief with clients were part of the job. I had a few coworkers to whom I would discuss how I felt, so I appreciate them for being there for me. Of course, I was not totally healed from grieving, but I reached a point of stomaching grief and confronting the grieving feelings to get total restoration from hurt. Besides, Momma needed me to help her get out of the dark grip that zapped a portion of life out of her. I had no idea of what her hurt and pain felt like to lose her child, her son, but I knew she was grieving beyond comprehension.

The loss of my brother was a *cut to the soul* for our family and for many who knew him. It was a *bitter* pill to swallow and a dark time that seemed not to have an ending. Our family had to relive the night that led to his death due to *Judas* who was arrested, and a trial occurred.

WDBJ7 or News 10 (cannot remember which news) interviewed me in front of the City of Martinsville Administration building. I had to take on an additional burden in spite of the grief that I felt, and that was the burden of my family. I knew my family would have to rely on my strength. One of my first cousins (father's niece) confirmed my thoughts by saying, "You know, you have to be strong for Peggy (my mom) and your aunt. If they see you breakdown, they will breakdown too."

Nevertheless, God who is merciful and full of grace got my family and me through the difficult time (court). I had prayed to God and said, "It does not matter how many years he (Judas) gets, I want the outcome to be a guilty verdict because he (Judas) is guilty. He murdered my brother."

I remember saying the same prayer in church on Sunday, the week leading to the court trial outcome; and within my spirit, I could hear a soft-sounding still voice say, "Guilty verdict." By faith, I held on to what I heard in my spirit and said, "God, I thank you for answering my prayer." The verdict result? You guessed correctly: *guilty*!

My brother, Spencer O'Neil Moyer

## CHAPTER 2

# *Remembering Momma*

My mother loved her family. Sometimes, I felt smothered by her love. For example, I experienced tightness in my chest as if a ton of bricks were on top of it. A minister who knew my mother told me (some time ago) that my mother *loved me from the womb*. Since her death, there have been many to tell me, "Your mother loved you and was proud of you."

I loved her as equally but not as a smothering type. We had become "you see one, you see the other." We went almost everywhere together. She became my shopping partner. If she had seen a pair shoes or clothing item she thought looked good on me after I tried it on, she asked, "Do you like it?"

If I say *yes* with a big grind, she'd say, "I will buy it for you." In my mother's eyes, I was her little girl regardless of my adult age. I was her little girl until the day she closed her eyes. Let me share what led to my mother's death. Come on, go on the journey with me to relive my experience. Are you ready? Let's go!

First I am proud to inform my mother was a hard worker too. She never turned to assistance from Social Services to take care of us. She worked and worked hard! She retired from working in the local furniture factory that no longer exists in the City of Martinsville. She taught me how to distinguish expensive furniture from less quality furniture. She knew if the furniture was actual cherrywood or pinewood. She educated me about how she marked wood for cutting and how to know if the wood was dry-rotted or good wood. Her laborer job as she describe it was "telling the machine in the rough end section." In other words, she would feed wood pieces into a machine.

My mother worked at three different well-known industrial industries in the Martinsville and Henry County area that are no longer in operation. She gave her 100 percent-plus to those factories. She was a dedicated employee who took pride in her work responsibilities for those factories. Her heart was broken and a sense of her dignity was robbed when the last factory (tenure was a little over five years) fired her while she was under doctor's care. She fought the unfair treatment of termination in spite of her medical condition. I was right by her side helping with getting important documents needed for her case. I assisted her with completing the paperwork to file her complaint with the Equal Employment Opportunity Commission (EEOC) in Virginia.

She did not win her case although as we perceived it, her complaint was legitimate in justifying the actions filed against the furniture company. The involvement of filing a complaint and following through with the process was a learning experience in which, together, my mother and I gave 100 percent. The fight was not in vain regardless of the outcome. In my opinion, life has a way of making things right, and this opinion is what I hold onto.

Nevertheless, a terminal illness invaded Momma's body for the second time. The first time Momma learned that she had colon cancer and shared the dreadful news with me was when I pulled in a parking space and was about to open the car door to attend a work meeting in Danville, Virginia. My cell phone rang, and Momma was on the other end. She called to inform me, "The doctor said that I have cancer."

I became numb and silent for a split second. I told her where I was and that I will come to her house once the meeting ended. I recall having a talk with God before I went inside to the meeting. I did not want to cry when sharing the news with the clinical director because I did not want others in attendance at the meeting to know what was happening. Therefore, before the meeting started, I whispered to the clinical director about the phone call from Momma. I felt like my world was crumbling, so I knew the news affected her even worse.

However, by God's loving grace, Momma had a fight in her. She went through radiation like a trooper. The radiation turned both palm of her hands and both bottom of her feet black. It look like smeared black paint. She experienced getting sores in her mouth, feeling sick and nausea, and went through a drastic diet change. I accompanied Momma to her scheduled doctor's appointments until she wanted to do it on her own. The oncologist marked the sight before doing the radiation treatment. When the radiation treatment ended, Momma took chemo medication, and the side effects that I witnessed her endure were not pleasant. Fortunately, the chemo medication prescribed did not cause her to have hair loss.

The cancer manifested a start of an educational journey that I could not forget. After Momma finished the cancer treatment, she received a bill of health. The doctor showed us the before-and-after pictures of her colon. Initially, the first cancerous colon picture was just that, a cancerous colon. The bill of health colon picture was pretty, pinkish, and looked healthy. Momma went back to working as a laborer and working part-time cleaning an office building in the City of Martinsville.

Unfortunately, five years later while vacationing in South Carolina at Myrtle Beach (fourth day at the beach), Momma revealed seeing blood in her stool. For a moment, we looked at one another, and she said, "I am not worrying this time. I leave it in God's hand."

I asked, "Is the bleeding bad?"

She responded, "Small amount on the tissue when I wiped."

I said, "We are calling the doctor when we get back to Virginia."

It was a Thursday evening, and we proceeded with our plans which was dinner, a movie (*Just Wright* starring Common and Queen Latifah), and riding to the south area of Myrtle Beach to sightsee. Momma showed no indications of worrying about what was happening in her body. She was strong, and I grew resiliently from observing how she dealt with unpleasant happenings in her life. She persisted in the midst of it all, and I withstood right along with her.

On the following Monday after our vacation, Momma contacted her doctor and scheduled an appointment. Of course, the test result was not surprising. The rectal cancer had returned, but this time, a stage four. The cancer was aggressive. The treatments started, decisions after decisions, and Momma elected to have surgery to remove a portion of her colon with the hopes that her butt would stop hurting. I was not agreeable about her decision and expressed it to her. She, with a frustrating look and snappy tone voice, said, "You don't know how bad my butt hurts!"

Truthfully, I had no idea. but deep down inside, I wanted her to change her mind. Why was I so adamant about her changing her mind? My thoughts were, *Once they open her up and air hits her insides, the cancer will spread.* Possibly, this could be a myth or maybe not, but the cancer spread to her pelvic area.

The spreading of the cancer to her pelvic area lead Momma to signing the Power of Attorney papers to give me authority over her medical treatment and overall affairs. The little girl in the eyes of Momma had to take on the role of being the mature and educated woman that I was. The caregiver role I faced was not always easy. Nevertheless, I treated Momma with the upmost respect. I considered her wishes regarding her desires because she was *my mother*, and in spite of the complex situation and my new responsibilities as a caregiver, she is Momma.

Due to the removal of a portion of Momma's colon, she had to wear a colonoscopy bag. Not only was I the caregiver, but I carried out the role of a nurse (how Momma started perceiving me). The hospital nurse taught me how to keep Momma's stoma clean, change the colonoscopy bag, and attach it to the stoma before the doctor discharged her home. The bag had to be changed often, and the great and astonishing part about this role, I *loved it*!

I rather change the colonoscopy bag than clean the wound that formed on Momma's rear-end because of the vicious cancer. Momma communicated to me in front of our neighbor, "Pheia like cleaning shit and rather change this bag than clean my wound." We laughed. I would clean the wound and bandage it as taught, but something about the colonoscopy bag was not a challenge but seen as an honorable duty. I knew it had to be God! Only God could make me strong mentally and give me the perspective that I had about the colonoscopy bag responsibility. Think for a moment. It stunk, and sometimes, the waste was runny like water, and sometimes the feces were solid. It took several tries before the correct colonoscopy bag fit Momma's stoma. Whew! Was not I glad when after a few colonoscopy manufacturing brands tried, the correct colonoscopy bags selected fitted her stoma. The relief of the colonoscopy bag leakage ended, but I constantly checking the bag did not stop because sometimes, Momma's feces were watery and leaked around the adhesion that sealed the colonoscopy bag attached to the stoma. In addition, the colonoscopy bag would fill up quickly with feces most times.

Momma's quality of life changed drastically. It got to the point that she could not go out the house because the cancer affected her pelvic area. The last outdoor activity with Momma was a ride on the back roads at her request. We had memorable moments talking about the areas located on the back roads. I recall before Momma's surgery to remove a portion of her colon getting a stool for her to sit on while she fixed a cake from scratch. I watched her as she gave all the strength she had to fix us a cake, and she kept saying to me, "You pay attention to how I am making this cake." I watched her. Could I duplicate her cake from scratch? No! Momma's *Kitchen Aid* mixer sits on the kitchen counter like a trophy.

Furthermore, she requested that I fix the potato salad. She guided me as I prepared to make the potato salad, and surprisingly, it turned out good! She praised me for fixing a good potato salad.

I said, "It is a lot of work in fixing a potato salad...I do not think that I would fix another one."

Of course, her response, "It's not all that much to fix potato salad."

I smiled and said, "Yes, it is too!"

She said, "You're just lazy."

I laughed and thought, *I am not trying to make another potato salad.* So far, I have not made another potato salad. I have bought some from the grocery store, though. God knows grocery store's potato salad is not the same as homemade.

Momma was an excellent cook and loved to cook for family, coworkers, and friends. She cooked homemade cakes, pies, cobblers, and big meals during holidays. She always cooked enough so that I could take home cook meals to eat at my house in the city. It did not have to be a holiday or a special occasion. When Momma cooked, she cooked plenty. She enjoyed cooking and watching the cooking shows. She got gratification out of seeing people eat her food and make over how good the food was.

Momma had heavy hands, meaning when she fixed a plate for you to eat, she piled the food on. One time during winter, I took a break from eating her cooking because I started putting on pounds. I am conscious of my weight. If I gain five pounds, I think it is too much and will not be satisfied about the weight gain until it is gone. Maybe you noticed that I took a journey detour, but we will get back on the voyage about Momma's bout with cancer.

There came to a point that Momma could not bear the pain. She walked some in the house, slept in the chair in the living room, or laid on the chase in the den area of the house before the colon surgery. She barely slept in her bed because she pained that bad and could not find comfort or relief. After the surgery and discharge from the hospital, Momma went straight to a nursing home but returned to the hospital on Thanksgiving Day due to her kidneys going into renal failure. Once she was discharge ready, the hospital social worker placed her in a different nursing home, and she remained there until meeting discharge status. All together between the two nursing homes, Momma spent about two months and a few days for rehabilitation care. While she was in the last nursing home, I moved out of my house in the city and moved into her home to get things ready for her. It was Christmas Day when Momma could come home for a day visit. She was not totally at the point in which the doctor and physical therapist saw her as discharge ready. I mixed some of my furniture with hers and had each room in the house looking beautiful, and this was her Christmas gift.

Therefore, when she came home for the Christmas Day visit, she knew I officially moved from my house and have come home.

Momma's desire was granted by God because she had always ask me, "When are you moving back home?"

I learned later that she and her neighbor had been praying that I would return home. Momma would say comments like, "You don't need to be staying in your house. You have a house. Move home and save your money."

Finally the time arrived for her discharge from the local nursing home. The staff at the last nursing home placement did a magnificent job in getting Momma stable to return home. They perceived her as a miracle because upon arrival to them, Momma was in a *bad shape*. Thank God for bouncing her back and answering prayers. Momma did not want to expire in the nursing home. She wanted to be home when the time comes for her to leave this world. I knew this and God too.

While living with Momma, I kept her toenails polished red (her color). One Saturday, we were in the den watching a program on television. And as I polished her toenails, I turned to look at her, and she was looking in the direction of the closet door. I saw the most beautiful smile on her face. She looked heavenly. I never mentioned the beautiful look that I saw on her face. She did not say anything about her encounter, either. The experience was as if she forgot that I was in the room with her, and it was her moment enjoying a supernatural encounter.

When *Whitney Houston* passed, Momma and I watched her homegoing service on television, and she cried and cried as if she knew it would eventually be her and I be alone. Before *President Barak Obama* ran a second term in office, Momma and I discussed about why he should get another term. I mentioned to her that I believed he would be reelected, but her enthusiasm was not there as it was when he initially ran for President of the United States. She looked at me and did not comment. I could feel that she knew she would not be around to see him be re-appointed although she said nothing. The look in her eyes said it all. The comment she did say was, "Pheia, he is of your generation." I responded *yes* and thought to myself, *She said this when he won president the first election.*

One time, I reached a breaking point moment caring for Momma. When you take on the only caregiver role because you are the only child, your life changes. The norm of things changes. My independence became at a halt. It hit me and hit me hard one Sunday when I was washing Momma's clothes, bed linens, and towels. I cried, and it was tears of frustration because I felt frustrated. I realized that a challenging shift has taken place in my life. My life was not as it was. Things have changed and changed quickly. No more going out when I wanted or going anywhere when I wanted. My life had become "take care of your momma and everything that involves her."

I cooked. I kept the house clean. I never wanted any visitors talking negatively about their visit with Momma when they left. Well, getting back to that particular Sunday, my neighbor happened to come over to check on Momma and me. My aunt was already visiting and come to see what she could do. I wanted to go to church because the last time going to church was at the last night youth revival service.

Oh, Lord! When I came home from the last night youth revival service, Momma was in the floor and softly saying in desperation, "Somebody help me." She had fell out the bed trying to get out of it when she heard a loud noise. She said, "It sounded like an airplane landing on the house. It was loud. Heard it twice."

My neighbor confirmed the next day that two military planes flew over the neighborhood. I realized then that Momma could not stay home alone for a few hours even if our neighbor checked on her. From that point on, Momma's experience of falling out the bed caused her to experience anxiety sometimes about walking. This was frustrating, and one time, she stopped and leaned against the wall in the hallway and would not take another step. I could not convince her that she will not fall. What ended up happening was, out of panic, I let go of her hand and bellowed, "I don't know what to do!" I caught her, and we both went down to the floor together. I called a neighbor to help me get her back in bed.

Therefore, to help give me some relief time, my aunt said she would watch my mom next Sunday so that I could attend church.

I went to church the next following Sunday, but I felt bad leaving Momma at home, and it did not matter knowing my aunt was there with her. Once, our neighbor's daughter-in-law came over on a Saturday so that I could leave the house for a while, but I chose to lie down and rest and did not really rest. I could not. I accepted that I could not have weekends for myself. My lot in life at that point is go to work. If I got a call from the certified nurse assistant (CNA) who managed Momma's care during the day, I handled the matter, get off work at 5:00 p.m., come home, and continue the duties where the CNA left off. Then repeat the same duties over. I felt blessed, and my prayer to have help coming in the home that I could trust was answered. I was relieved knowing Momma was safe while I was at work. My aunt was a blessing to Momma and me. She supported financially compensating the CNA.

I remember getting a pedicure and feeling guilty. I knew the guilt feeling surfaced because Momma could not come along and get the same pampering. Monthly, I would show Momma how I spent her social security check. I never used her money for my personal use. I worked, so I spent my money, and I felt extremely good for not spending her money and doing *right* by her. I know this is why I can stay in my inherited home and occasionally sleep in the room where she passed because my conscious is clear. Thank you, Jesus!

The dreadful time finally came when I had to get Momma to accept hospice care. It had gotten to the point that she frequently needed to see her oncologist or visit the emergency room. I explained to her that the hospice nurse would do regular home visits and if she needed anything to assist with making her comfortable, the nurse provides the care. And she would not have to leave home to get medicine or intravenous fluids from her oncologist or the emergency room. Momma agreed and refused to use the oxygen provided through hospice care. She allowed me to give her oxygen once, and the next time I tried, she stated, "You are hardheaded. I told you that I do not need the oxygen, Pheia. You are hardheaded." I never gave her oxygen after that episode, and she did not need it. Momma did fine without it.

From the time of Momma's discharge from the nursing home January, 2012, on up to the last three weeks of her life, her health did not steadily decline until the last three weeks of her life on earth. She became bedridden, but her mind was sharp. I can remember her sharing with me about seeing a dark figure in her room and showing me where she saw it. She could describe the dark figure in detail. She said, "It was black dark. It had no eyes, and I could not see my hands." She uttered, "I saw it come through the window, and why is this and what is it?"

I knew what the figure was, and I did not want it in her room either. To make her feel better, I let up the window and commanded the dark figure to *go in Jesus's name and not to return*. Then I let the window down after giving the command. She appeared relieved and for a few days slept well at night.

What I learned was when that figure would enter her room, Momma would hold her arms up in the air in the form of a cross. The cross Momma made with her arms would let me know that she suspected it was death too. How I knew this was when I would hear her make a noise as if she was fighting something off, so I peeked into her room. The experience she encountered happened about twice as far as I know because I heard her fighting sounds two times. And both times, I glanced into her room and saw her arms in the air in a cross position. Lastly when we were eating breakfast one morning, she said, "Hang up blinds at the kitchen windows because people looking."

My response was, "No one can see us."

Her reply was, "Yes, they can too."

During that time, Momma could walk some in the house but did not have enough strength to go outside the house and go some-where. Two of the kitchen windows have no blinds, but swags were hanging. Besides, the two kitchen windows face the back of the house. I have yet to hang up blinds.

Additionally, prior to Momma becoming bedridden, she told the hospice nurse and the CNA who provided care during the day, "I see Jesus in Pheia's bedroom when she walked past it." She verbalized seeing Jesus to them twice. The hospice nurse alerted me that *when-*

*ever a hospice patient start talking about him or her seeing Jesus, it is only a matter of time that he or she is getting ready to die.*

The second week on a weekend of the third week approaching, Momma looked at me as if to say, "When are you taking time off from work?" I understood her message loud and clear. When I went to work Monday, I went to human resources (HR) to get the Family Medical Leave Act (FMLA) papers and brought them home to complete with intent to submit them to HR that week which was the third week. I thought, *I'd submit the papers Friday.*

Momma and I spoke mainly with our eyes to one another during certain occurrences that were overwhelming to discuss. For instance, after the surgery from which the doctor removed a portion of her colon, I could not relate to her that the surgery was considered not successful because the doctor learned the cancer had spread to her pelvic. The doctor informed she would live about six months. Momma and my eyes connected, and she knew it was not good news.

Anyway, back to the third week, it was Thursday and I left my cell phone at home. Usually, I put my cell phone in my pocketbook before leaving the house. Therefore, I went home during lunchtime to get my phone. When I got there, Momma seemed not talkative and alert, but I kept talking to her anyway. The CNA informed that Momma had been like that all day. She called the hospice nurse, and the nurse came to check on Momma and indicated that her vitals were low, but she was not at the point of expiring. Momma would not take her medicine, eat, or drink. She did recognize my voice and tried to talk before I left to return to work. I told her that I love her, and she tried to say she love me too. I reached down and kissed her, and she mustard up strength to kiss me back. I felt an odd feeling like it was death on her, and I shared that with a coworker. But I did not say the word *death.* Instead, I spelled it out. Throughout the rest of the workday, I was bothered about the encounter with Momma when I went home for lunch.

When I got home from work, I had a reflection about the weekend and remembering seeing a heavenly glow encasing around the house. It looked like white clouds opened with golden sunrays shinning from it down on the house. I indicate it encased the house because it appeared to cover the front part of the house. I could see this supernatural sight from the living room front door when I turned and looked in that direction. When it happened, I was in the kitchen washing dishes. The living room and the kitchen faced each other, so I can see the living room door. I was not frightened but felt a calmness over me. Momma was pretty much in the same condition. She did not respond to her sister who came over later that evening. I shared with her what the hospice nurse said about Momma's vitals. I mentioned to my aunt about Momma not taking her medicine, eating, or drinking today; and she was doing the same this evening.

I did not sleep too well that night because of checking on Momma most of the night to see if she was breathing. Finally I drifted off to sleep, and it seemed like morning came fast. It was Friday April 20, 2012. I began to pray, and when lifting Momma up in prayer, it was as if I could not pray. I checked on her and noticed she was still breathing, so I showered and dressed. I called her name several times, but she would not respond. I called the hospice nurse telling her Momma is breathing but not responding, and she said, "I will be right over." She did not live too far away, just out the road a little ways.

When the hospice nurse arrived, she checked Momma's vitals and informed her vitals were fading. She said, "Call the family." So I called my aunt who was at work at the barbershop and maternal uncle who lived slightly up the road, his house in view from Momma's home. My uncle is now deceased (passed September 26, 2017).

I called our pastor, Alan Preston, and he came immediately. He got to Momma's house before my aunt and uncle. The CNA who took care of her had arrived and doing light cleaning in the house. She put in Momma's favorite gospel CD in the television/video player while I held her hand, rubbing her hand, and calmly saying, "Momma, I love you." Pastor Preston let her know he was in the room. I told Pastor, "I called my aunt, and she said, 'I am coming.' And it was about twenty minutes ago."

Then I heard a knock at the kitchen door. I said to Pastor "that's auntie" while I was going to unlock the door. Well, it was not my aunt. It was no one at the door. I went back to Momma's bedside and told Pastor, "It was not my aunt, and no one was at the door."

I proceeded holding Momma's hand and rubbing her hand. Then suddenly, Momma's eyes looked straight up toward the direction of the television/video player. I could hear a sound like something was moving, but the sound was not a car, train, airplane, boat, or wind sound. The sound seemed peaceful in my ears but powerful enough to pull Momma forward toward it. Pastor Preston touched me lightly on my arm and said, "Look, look!"

We both witnessed Momma's legs raising from the bed and her legs *raised* from the bed straight. Next her face turned toward me, and her eyes closed as if she went to sleep. Precious in the sight of the Lord is the death of his saints (Psalm 116:15). Momma expired early morning (9:00 a.m.) without a struggle. She passed peacefully.

"And I said, Oh that I had wings like a dove! For then would I fly away, and be at rest" (Psalm 55:6). She accepted her wings and took her rest.

Another astonishing occurrence was God healed Momma. None of her body fluids were on the bedsheets. Her wound dried up. The only odor left behind was the *death smell,* but it went away after letting the windows up for a few hours. The fresh air came through the windows and took it away. Momma was a proud woman. She loved to smell good and look nice. God made sure that her passing did not leave her body fluids behind to clean up, and that was amazing!

My aunt arrived after Momma passed. I told her about the knock at the door and thinking it was her, but it was not. I said to auntie, "The angel came." I continued to say, "At least the angel knocked, but I was not given the option of letting him in or not." I sort of smile, for I saw humor in my remark. After all what could I do, it was beyond my control.

However, the experience of seeing how Momma passed was like none other. I saw death in a different perspective. Oddly, my thought was, *Death is beautiful.* At the burial site, I performed the committal part of the service, and that was an honor. Momma was buried next to her son, my brother Spencer O'Neil Moyer as she requested. Actually, Momma was buried at the feet of Spencer.

My momma, Lula Mae "Peggy" Griggs Moyer

# CHAPTER 3

# My Experiences

Somehow, during childhood, I was captivated about having some sort of phenomenal powers. I do believe it stemmed from the famous memorable television shows *I Dream of Jeannie, Bewitched,* and *The Munsters.* Although I was fully aware that these three shows were a figurative of imaginations, they had my curiosity searching for wanting to perform like the characters. I viewed the horoscope and astrology as a way to connect to power and read it often. The *Magic 8 Ball* fascinated me because it was another source of power, but the *Ouija board* game frightened me, and I would not play it. I remember playing the *Magic 8 Ball* game with childhood friends and something entered the room and turned the doorknob while we were asking it questions. Terrified, we looked at one another while calling each other's name. And in sincerity and fright, we asked God to forgive us! Hastily, *Magic 8 Ball* became history!

Moreover, in spite of my quest for power, I have no idea where I got the information about "running around the outside of your house ten times when it is dark, look up into the sky, and you would see Satan." Of course, my curiosity got the best of me because I did what I learned about how to see Satan. At age ten on a hot summer night, I ran around the outside of my house ten times. When I got to the back of the house on count ten, I looked toward the left direction upward. And lo and behold, I saw a man's face. His face appeared slender and scaly (skeleton bones in his face structure) and shined like a full moon. The shininess of his face camouflaged the skeleton look but was noticeable enough for me to know I saw what appears to be bones. The hair on his head looked like thick waves of ocean water, and it was a charcoal deep black color, and the goatee hanging from his chin in a pointed shape was the same color too! His stern, lifeless eyes seemed to pierce right through me as if to entice or charm me. The Second Epistle (letter) of Apostle Paul to Corinthians comments, "And no marvel; for Satan himself is transformed into an angel of light" (2 Corinthians 11:14). In other words, as I interpret, Satan comes to deceive and is a deceiver. Fearful by the experience, I told God, "I want do that ever again." The man's face seen in the night sky supposedly been Satan was an imprinted photograph in my memory and thankful to God it did not scare me because it has no barren and has no power over me.

Besides, I found the power that I was searching for at age sixteen, and that power is the Holy Ghost (Holy Spirit). I was baptized at age fifteen, a week before my sixteenth birthday in November. I remember the preacher saying, "I baptize you in the name of the Father, the Son, and the Holy Ghost in Jesus's name." Acts 2:38 (KJV) indicates, "Then Peter said unto them, 'Repent, and be baptized every one of you in the name of Jesus Christ for the remission of sins, and ye shall receive the gift of the Holy Ghost.'" Glory to God! I repented of my sins, invited Christ into my life, and from that point on, my life gradually started changing. 2 Corinthians 5:17 (KJV), Apostle Paul wrote, "Therefore, if any man be in Christ, he is a new creature: old things have passed away; behold all things are become new." I began seeing a new me developing with different perspectives about life, situations, observations, and perception of me.

Additionally, at age sixteen, I was attending a Sunday evening service, and the preacher was preaching about the Holy Ghost. He let the congregation know that "the Holy Ghost is a gift, all you have to do is believe, and you will be filled." I believed and received the filling of the Holy Spirit with the evidence of speaking in tongues (unknown language). "And they were filled with the Holy Ghost and

began to speak with other tongues as the Spirit gave them utterance"
(Acts 2:4, KJV).

My relationship with Christ grew to levels after levels and
growth in him continues. It was later in my walk with Christ that
I learned to denounce occult-type practices. As a child, I was clue-
less about practices such as astrology, Ouija Boards, Magic 8 Ball,
and the like were considered evil although the neighborhood senior
saints warned that these practices are contrary to the Word of God.
My mother did not practice these things. I viewed the phenomenon
practices as mysterious fun that do not harm.

Autonomy, I believe, is the door to my curiosity and discoveries.
I, independently, was seeking who I am, where do I fit, and what do
I want to be. My main attraction was entertainment (be a *star*!) and
a fashion model. Growing up listening to the Jackson-5 music, doing
their dance moves, watching their television shows, reading about
their life in magazines, and having almost every girl's dream—"marry
Michael Jackson" attracted me. Likewise, Soul Train—the dancers
and guest performers—and loved *Seventeen* magazines captivated
me, so I could not envision anything else but desiring the limelight
they portrayed.

On another note, Momma called me *bossy* whenever I tell others what to do, including her, but only to a certain degree would
she allow me to boss her. When she gave me *the eye* (the look that
indicated "I am your momma, pull it together"), I knew how to
straighten up. My mother never whooped me but one time. I always
got *the eye* from her. I think I was five years old when Momma
whooped me for peeing in my pants because she warned me not to
do this. Apparently, I had peed in my clothes more than once. My
aunt was at the family field that was within eye distance of our family
home playing softball with her age group of neighborhood friends.
Therefore, when Momma started whooping me, I broke away and
ran to the front porch of the family home. Momma got ahold of me
before I could get off the porch and continued whooping my butt. I
knew if my aunt saw Momma beating me and hearing me screaming,
she would rescue me.

Momma was upset with me for peeing in my pants. She whooped my behind with a short plank. My aunt rescued me too! I did not pee in my clothes anymore after that whooping. I really believed that my feelings were hurt more so than getting the whooping. You see, I grew up in an extended family home (Momma, aunt, and grandfather) and lived with them until Momma bought a home in the neighborhood eye distance from the family home. My auntie and grandfather (deceased) let me get by with everything. "Pheia can't do no wrong," Momma would say. Auntie and grandpa favored me!

When grandpa's sister (deceased) visited us, I would jump up and down on the bed knowing she did not like me doing this. She told me on one of her visits, "I will whoop you if you don't stop jumping on the bed!"

Grandpa told her, "No, you won't. Come here, Toni." Toni is the nickname Grandpa gave me from the day that I was born into this world, and he never called me by my birth name. For a long time, I called him *Daddy* before calling him *Grandpa*. I was in the seventh grade before I started addressing him as Grandpa. I remember the first time that I called him Grandpa, I felt ashamed and struggled at saying *Grandpa* too. I have no clue as to why I felt ashamed, but the more I addressed him as Grandpa, the easier it became to say *Grandpa,* and the embarrassing feeling eventually alleviated and went away.

As I got older advancing from milk to meat, I learned more about occult-type practices and how such rituals are not God's will for anyone's life. The Bible indicates "the word of God is quick, and powerful, and sharper than any two-edged sword, piercing even to the dividing asunder of soul and spirit, and of the joints and marrow, and is a discerner of the thoughts and intents of the heart" (Hebrews 4:12).

My life and life's perceptions were changing. My way of thinking was quickly progressing wisely. While residing in Norfolk, Virginia, sitting under astute teachings, I learned about occult practices. And during that time, the television evangelist Pat Robertson of *The 700 Club* enlightened me about such ungodly customs also. God knows (grinning inwardly) expounding on the occult would be another book to write!

Furthermore, I recollect at age sixteen when it was summer and school out. I laid down to nap before going to hang out with friends in the City of Martinsville. I mentioned Momma's four-door light blue Ford Falcon in Chapter 1, but at age sixteen, I began calling it *the boat* and liked driving it too! While napping, I was awaken by the sounds of wings clapping, and I saw a vision of thick pure white huge wings with a white long flowing gown-look land on the back of Momma's Falcon. The pure white wings were so thick that a person could hide behind them and no one would know. In the vision, I did not see the full length of the figure with wings only the figure's backside from waist down land on the rear end of Mom's car. Instantly, I knew the figure was an angel! My guardian angel!

The angel rested on the back of my mom's car to protect me because when I went to my friends' (two sisters) home in the city, we were leaving to go hang out with our friends at the parking lot adjacent to Albert Harris Elementary School (gathering spot for teens) when I discovered the car had no brakes. As I backed out my friends' driveway, I mashed the brakes to change gear from reverse to drive. The brakes were loose, and the brake pedal went down to the floor.

Immediately, I hit the park brakes, and the car stopped. Thank God! The angel apparently remained on the back of the car because not once did the brakes give out while driving to my friends' home. To get to the main road from my house, there is a steep hill to go down, and there are curves and a hill before getting to my friends' house. "For he shall give his angels charge over thee, to keep thee in all thy ways" (Psalm 91:11). I am convinced that God sent the angel not only to watch over me but also to protect me.

## CHAPTER 4

# *Revealing Dreams*

> And God said, "Let us make man in our image, after our likeness: and let them have dominion over the fish of the sea, and over the fowl of the air, and over the cattle, and over all the earth, and over every creeping thing that creepeth upon the earth.' So God created man in his own image, in the image of God created he him; male and female created he them." (Genesis 1:26–27, KJV)

Because humanity was made in the image of God, according to the Bible, it makes humankind unique from the creation of animals and the rest of creation itself. Therefore, man formed in three parts and the three parts are spirit, soul (mind), and body. The body house the spirit and soul while it is on earth. The Apostle Paul in 1 Thessalonians 5:23 (KJV) wrote, "And the very God of peace sanctify you wholly; and I pray God your whole spirit and soul and body be preserved blameless unto the coming of our Lord Jesus Christ."

In view of this, we know the body is man's physical side that can be touched, embraced, hugged, and gratified. But the spirit and the soul cannot because these are our emotions, will, intellect, and conscience. The Apostle Paul writing in Roman 12:2 (KJV) instructs, "And be not conformed to this world: but be ye transformed by the renewing of your mind, that ye may prove what is that good, and acceptable, and perfect, will of God."

Hebrews 4:12, as mentioned in Chapter 3, is befitting to reiterate once more because it describes the Word of God as "piercing even to the dividing asunder of soul and spirit, and of the joints and marrow, and is a discerner of the thoughts and intents of the heart." I view Hebrews 4:12 as confirming that the Word of God *piercing* the heart causes the soul and spirit to divide in which only God can perform such act.

For that reason, this leads me to dreaming. The Word of God informs that God is mindful of man and visits him, made him a little lower than the angels, crowned him with glory and honor, and set him over the works of thy hands (Hebrew 2:6–7). The Bible consists of indications where God revealed his *will* through communicating to particular ones by way of dreams. For instance:

> But while he thought on these things, behold, the angel of the Lord appeared unto him in a dream, saying, "Joseph, thou son of David, fear not to take unto thee Mary thy wife: for that which is conceived in her is of the Holy Ghost." (Mathew 1:20, KJV)

Another example:

> And when they were departed, behold, the angel of the Lord appeareth to Joseph in a dream, saying, "Arise, and take the young child and his mother, and flee into Egypt, and be thou there until I bring thee word: for Herod will seek the young child to destroy him." (Mathew 2:13, KJV)

Of course, in the Bible, there are other occasions where God spoke to selected ones through dreams (e.g., Genesis 37:5–10; 1Kings 3:5–15).

Today I believe God continues to speak to us through dreams for it is evident in both the Old and New Testaments.

> And it shall come to pass afterward, that I will pour out my spirit upon all flesh; and your sons and your daughters shall prophesy, your old men shall dream dreams, your young men shall see visions. (Joel 2:28; Acts 2:17, KJV)

Nevertheless, it behooves us to seek God about every vivid dream or dreams that have repetitive occurrences (dreams that seem to disturb us or cannot depart from our mind). Our thoughts can get distant from us (produce trickeries), and Satan can present bogus deceptions to our thoughts as well. So turning to God for understanding about our dreams will keep us from leaning to our own understanding as we interpret dreams.

Now that the preliminaries are out of the way, I would like to take you on two *revealing dreams* in which I have dreamt. The dreams I am about to divulge are interesting and useful for great discussions. Let us grab a cup of coffee, tea, hot chocolate, or whatever beverage consumption preferred that jumpstarts your day and listen attentively at my dreams. I suggest that you have paper and pen ready to jot your thoughts as my dreams reveal your interpretations for a dissecting conversation. Remember, my dreams are an interchanging dialogue tool for you.

I recall a dream in which I associate with salvation. The dream occurred in the late 1980s. I rededicated my life to the Lord consciously and with a wholehearted mind believing he is my life and my salvation and without him, I would fail. The Bible tells us we can do nothing apart from God (John 15:5). No longer did I desire to live in a backslide state. I had enough Word of God in me to know that he is married to the backslider. So repenting of my sins, I returned to the Lord, and he accepted me back. The major prophet Jeremiah's words from the Lord spoken to Israel and Judah in their backslidden condition verify that God *is* married to the backslider. "Turn, O backsliding children, saith the LORD; for I am married unto you:

and I will take you one of a city, and two of a family, and I will bring you to Zion" (Jeremiah 3:14, KJV).

Okay, so in this particular dream, I was between two places. I could see below me what appeared to look like a dungeon (cold and dreary). I could see demons! The demons were grayish in color, and there were several of them. They were making a noise that I could not distinguish, but I knew in my mind that they were after my soul. The demons' faces were scaly and shaped like a lizard with a human body form that was scaly too. It appeared that they were surrounding a master demon who gave orders, and their orders were to take my soul. Remember, I was between two places, so above me was a bright shining light shined downward toward me. I could feel the bright light pull me upward before the demons clutched my soul. When I awoke from the vivid dream, I knew that Jesus Christ saved me. And no one could tell me anything different. I belonged to Christ and fully knew within my heart that I am his. Satan could not have me, and God made it clear through the dream.

On June 6, 2017, the clock on the nightstand in my bedroom showed 3:37 a.m. I reached for my pen and pad to write what I had dreamt. The sounds of hearing what sounded like airplanes flying low but turned out to be numerous of torpedoes falling from the sky several at a time that I was unable to count awakened me from my sleep. The torpedoes were gray with a black five-point star outlined in white, and the torpedoes looked like military weapons. In the dream, there were men dressed in army uniforms (infantry uniforms and fighter uniforms, my interpretation). Some of the men looked like Americans, and some looked like Japanese men dressed in white T-shirts and dressed pants that looked military style. I saw one helicopter with no door facing me from its left side. There were two men (black) seated in the front section of the helicopter and a lady seated at the back of the helicopter had on a white sweater and a long black-and-white skirt (quarter length), and she was hiding her face and would not look in my direction. However, I saw the side of her, but her hair covered that side of her face. Oddly, I was thinking in the dream that the woman was First Lady *Michelle Obama*: The

Obamas! As a figure of speech, I say to you, to me while smiling, "Go figure, right?"

When the torpedoes hit the ground, they did not explode. They were still intact, but there were so many that fell from the sky and landed on the ground. Those torpedoes were released from warplanes that could not be seen but heard (noise was loud!). Not only I who was in the dream saw what was happening, but many on the ground witnessed it too. Prior to the torpedoes falling from the sky or the sound of military planes being heard, I was saying to the people as well as three friends from high school, "America needs to pray and to start praying constantly asking God to forgive us and heal our land to protect us."

I said the statement twice before the sounds of warplanes (could not be seen) started dropping torpedoes (gray with a black five-point star outlined in white). In the dream while I was saying the statement, a woman about my age appeared to look and said, "I saw a black sign in the sky." She interpreted it as death. The black sign hovered over America. Then I repeated the statement a second time. "America needs to pray and to start praying constantly asking God to forgive us and heal our land to protect us." And soon after saying the statement for the second time, the torpedoes started falling from the sky.

The torpedoes appeared like fireworks on a July 4th. In the dream, I used my iPhone to take pictures. When I took a picture of the helicopter and those inside it, I remember saying to myself, "Don't let them see you taking pictures." Lastly in this dream, I recall those on the ground were going about doing routine things in life such as taking pictures of each other to post on social media and in bars drinking and socializing. I even requested a picture to be taken of the two high school friends and I and asked the third high school friend to get in the picture.

Finally it is puzzling about high school people showing up in this dream and a second picture taken of one of the high school friends, myself, and two other women whose faces I could not see well but knew they attended the same high school. In the picture of us, we had on blue jeans; and our pose was sideways slightly showing the backside of us. The dream, to me, was filled with many metaphors. And I considered researching the dream color meanings since they seemingly have a repetitive significance. It is possible that the dream has a political meaning and the indication that there will be another war, a war of nuclear artillery, which will force America to her knees and cry out to God for help. No one can hide. Everyone can be affected by the *terror* that will come upon the land.

## CHAPTER 5

# *Spirit Travels*

Supernaturally, the spirit in us can travel. There is information that points to the *spirit travels* when we are at rapid eye movement (REM) sleep or deep sleep. Telepathy is another form in which our spirit can travel. Telepathy occurs when our consciousness separates from the physical body and travels outside it. Telepathy, in my opinion, is a method I rather not indulge in because I view it as tapping into a dimension that is ungodly, occultism. Extrasensory perception (ESP) is a term associated with telepathy as well.

However, a true worshiper of God will worship him in spirit and in truth. In John 4:23–24 (KJV) are the words of Jesus stating, "But the hour cometh and now is, when the true worshippers shall worship the Father in spirit and in truth: for the Father seeketh such to worship him. God is a Spirit: and they that worship him must worship him in spirit and in truth."

John 4:23–24 is the supporting Scripture that explains an encounter of my spirit traveling when I attended TV evangelist Joyce Myers conference a few years ago at the Lawrence Joel Veterans Memorial Coliseum in Winston Salem, North Carolina.

During the conference, a video *Hand of Hope* was shown. And afterward, the volunteers passed buckets in the aisles for everyone to give an offering for that mission. After the money was collected, an offertory prayer was prayed, and I asked God to increase my $20 gift given. Immediately, I felt my spirit traveling and could see it travel over a body of water that looked like the sea stretching for miles, no land seen; and within my heart, I knew the body of water was international waters. I was not sleeping, so it was not a dream experienced. I was awake, praying, touching, and agreeing about the prayer prayed over the funds collected for *Hand of Hope*. But supernaturally, my spirit traveled, and I felt it traveling and saw where it was roaming.

Another occasion in which my spirit traveled was during a workweek in January 2017. Oh how I remember this frightening yet peaceful occurrence. I awoke from my sleep by what seemingly startled me was a heavy presence on my bed that caused me to start fighting for my life. In that fight, my spirit traveled to a place that I knew was the *belly of hell*. I could see numerous of people in shadow form inside of flames and hear the people crying out "Jesus save us!"

I could feel a fear that words cannot describe and feel an unrest that was indescribable. Then my spirit traveled upward, and as it traveled upward, I could sense peace—calmness—and I could see a man surrounded by beautiful clouds as he looked down toward the people on earth. No white color on earth could match the white color of those clouds! I felt safe and secure in the man's presence. Then I came to myself. *I came to myself* means my spirit came back into my body. I remember saying instantly, "Lord, I don't want to go to hell."

Pondering the experience and sharing it with a few people had me desiring an understanding of what happened to me and what God was saying. Those whom I shared the experience gave their input, but one person sought God and felt possibly that Psalm 14:1–5 affirmed my supernatural traveling experience.

> The fool hath said in his heart, "There is no God." They are corrupt, they have done abominable works, there is none that doeth good. The LORD looked down from heaven upon the children of men, to see if there were any that did understand, and seek God. They are all gone aside, they are all together become filthy: there is

none that doeth good, no, not one. Have all the
workers of iniquity no knowledge? who eat up
my people as they eat bread, and call not upon
the LORD. There were they in great fear: for
God is in the generation of the righteous. (Psalm
14:1–5, KJV)

After reading Psalm 14:1–5, which was not my first time reading it; but this time, I saw the significant meaning and believed the
clarification came from the Holy Spirit. The supernatural traveling
of my spirit in regards to Psalm 14:1–5 refers to the evildoers as the
ones who were in the belly of hell crying out *Jesus!* The Word of God
lets us know that "every knee should bow and every tongue should
confess that Jesus is LORD!"

That at the name of Jesus every knee should bow,
of things in heaven, and things in earth, and
things under the earth; And that every tongue
should confess that Jesus Christ is Lord, to the
glory of God the Father. (Philippians 2:10–11)

The evildoers seen in the belly of hell were overwhelmed with
dread. Perhaps the existing evil doers are doing the same, crying out
for relief. But perhaps, their cries are going out to a false god who
cannot deliver. As a result, they carry out harm in the name of their
false god hoping to obtain peace. Probably, their act of violence is
temporary (in the moment of their actions) and still no inner peace
within their souls. While in the *belly of hell*, my spirit experienced
the horrifying fear and unrest the evildoers are chain to for eternity.
Therefore, when my spirit traveled downward into the *belly of hell* to
be a witness as to what was going on with humankind in life after
death, God was in the midst of me. Wow! He is an *awesome* God!
Who can phantom or know the mind of God? How I perceive it is
what he chooses to do or who he selects to use on this earth to get his
message across to us is his sovereign choice.

Last of all, it could be that you have a different explanation concerning the divine experience I shared and if so, that is good. I encourage you to discuss your views with others. Learn what others think with an open mind. Explore the scripture indicated and every supporting scriptures that may be a reference to Psalm 14:1–5. I do not know, but my supernatural encounter could make an intriguing Bible study for you individually or with a group (smile).

# CHAPTER 6

# *Listen*

Working in the human services profession has taught me to practice active listening. "So what is active listening?" you may perhaps ask. My definition of active listening is listening beneath the surface to know exactly what a person is saying from the depths of his or her heart. In other words, you can discern what the person intends to verbalize or needs to verbalize when he or she does not. The person does not reveal his or her authentic feelings or thoughts when the two of you are discussing his or her concerns. The person converses with you in riddles or with difficulty expressing him or herself.

Additionally, after reading several definitions about active listening, I thought that I would compile and write a brief summation definition. *Active listening is a skill and communication technique that is achieved through full concentration about something said and not two or more people hearing inactively between the exchanging of conversations.* This type of active listening necessitates demonstration of attentiveness and empathy to effectively respond, paraphrase, and comprehend to one another.

However, I ask you to ponder this question, "Does active listening transmits in the same manner between spiritual people versus unspiritual people?" For instance, I recall that when I was a teenager, my maternal aunt and I went to Stuart, Virginia, to visit her mother's sister. I never met my maternal aunt and my mother's mother. She passed away from breast cancer when Momma and her siblings were children. It was articulated to me that "she had mental problems." I was told, "She had business about herself too" (meaning she knew how to acquire things such as land).

Well, my aunt's aunt whom we visited in Stuart, Virginia, had a dark-skin complexion. She was a thin elderly woman with arm-length natural grayish-white hair platted in two plats. The white hair edges around her front hairline was fuzzy and curly looking. She would say to us, "Be quiet. Be quiet. The Lord is speaking." I had no idea of why she said that and neither did my aunt. My aunt and I would get quiet and look at one another. And when we left her house, our conversation was something is wrong with her, and we'd laugh. But internally, I was concerned and felt my aunt was too. I think how I arrived at this conclusion as a teenager was due to her home. It was a small, possibly four-room white wood house that appeared dark inside. There was a wood stove in the front entrance of the house. She spoke softly as we talked, and the smile on her face indicated she was happy to see us. I viewed her house as a historical home—a sturdy home built from solid wood by maybe another family member, "I don't know!" Her home, as I saw it, reminded me of slaves' living quarters on a plantation! Her style of dress was not modern but old fashion like the old-fashioned attire I have seen church members who attend the same church as I wear on Old Fashion Day.

Nevertheless, as I grew closer to God, I understood that God does speak to you. Sometimes, it is supernaturally (hear a small still voice within your spirit or heart), or he speaks many other ways such as a sermon heard in church, something read in the Bible, or non-biblical readings, inspirational or secular movies, inspiring plays, or through conversations from other people. God can speak to you in dreams or visions—from quotes and others shared that developed from their life experiences. In addition, you can hear God speaking from something you read on a billboard or a sign hanging inside or outside a public building. What I am implying or attempting to convey is, God speaks to us however he chooses. There is no restriction as to how he speaks to us. Since God speaks to us in various ways, what should we do to hear him? The answer is we too must practice active listening with God to hear him.

Therefore, to hear him is to know him; and to know him is to develop a relationship with him. Jeremiah 29:11 (KJV) says, "'For I know the thoughts that I think toward you,' saith the Lord, 'thoughts of peace, and not of evil, to give you an expected end.'"

Similarly, God demonstrates active listening to us as well. Jeremiah 29:11 is letting us know "*God has our best interest at heart,*" which is a common phrase that is not new to us. Whenever we find it difficult to express how we feel about something because of believing our perceptions are right and others are not, this could indicate that we are not right and should revisit our point of views. If we have no peace about our perceptions and we continue fishing for the right points to validate our observations, this is another indicator that our perceptions need revisiting. Remember, God sees directly into our hearts. "Every way of a man is right in his own eyes: but the LORD pondereth the hearts" (weighs the hearts) (Proverbs 21:2).

Accordingly, how do we hear from God? We can hear from him by praying, reading the Word of God, having daily devotions, discussing his Word at Bible study and Sunday school meetings, and through others. These are a few ways to hear his voice. Having a conversation with him as if you would with your spouse, parents, siblings, coworkers, relatives, neighbors, friends, and strangers are ways to hear him as well. Practice stillness from the daily bustle, routines, and attending this function and that function helps with hearing from God. You know what distracts you. No one needs to tell you. Who could tell you better than you tell yourself "I need to remove myself from distractions!"? I suggest that you identify your distractions, call them by name, and do what you should to get rid of them, so you can hear clearly from God.

Proverbs 3:5–6 (KJV) encourages us to "Trust in the LORD with all thine heart; and lean not unto thine own understanding. In all thy ways acknowledge him, and he shall direct thy paths." Daily recognition of the Lord is valuable to you existing. Acknowledge that he exits by letting him know you are thankful for all he does for you. Recognize that it is him who woke you up this morning, giving you strength to carry out your daily routines, showing you how to resolve issues as they arise, releasing angels to watch over you, and so forth. When you put God first before starting your day, you will know when he is speaking to you.

Jacob wrestled with a man until the breaking of day and called the place Peniel, meaning he saw God face-to-face and was spared (Genesis 32:22–32). During the struggle as indicated in Genesis 32:22–32, Jacob had a conversation with the man he called God, and the man asked him, "What is your name?' He said *Jacob*, and the man changed Jacob's name to Israel, meaning *for a prince has power with God and with men and have prevailed.*

Think about it. How could Jacob have prevailed and received a name change if he had not interacted with the man he called God? How could Jacob have realized he was in a battle, not only from his hip getting out of joint but also from knowing he had seen the face of God? My interpretation is that Jacob had a divine encounter with an *angel* sent by God to be transparent before him. The *angel* appearing before Jacob in the form of a man who wrestled with him until the breaking of day indicates that Jacob would know God is with him, leading him, guiding him, and directing him. Lastly the name change signified a specific transformation occurred with Jacob (old man, forgiven to a new man, converted).

Jacob arrived at a point in his life that he had to face his brother Esau for taking (stealing by trickery) Esau's birthright (Genesis 27:1–29). Jacob, wrestling with the man, prepared to meet his brother after many years of the two not seeing one another. Jacob fled to his maternal uncle's home in Haran after he stole Esau's birthright because Esau was angered; enough to kill him (Genesis 28:41–44).

Even while Jacob was on the run, the Lord spoke to him through a dream. Jacob dreamed a ladder set on the earth, and the top of it reached to heaven: and behold the angels of God ascending and descending on it.

> And, behold, the LORD stood above it, and said,
> "I am the LORD God of Abraham, thy father,
> and the God of Isaac: the land whereon thou

liest, to thee will I give it, and to thy seed. And
thy seed shall be as the dust of the earth, and thou
shalt spread abroad to the west, and to the east,
and to the north, and to the south: and in thee
and in thy seed shall all the families of the earth
be blessed. And, behold, I am with thee, and will
keep thee in all places whither thou goest, and
will bring thee again into this land; for I will not
leave thee, until I have done that which I have
spoken to thee of." (Genesis 28:13–15, KJV)

The story of Jacob lets us know that God will speak to us in
the midst of our dark times, complicated times, distressing times,
and bleak times. God loves us enough to let us know he is with us
in spite of our wrongs. If God has a plan for your life, it will come
forth, but you have to acknowledge he has a plan. After the prophetic
dream, "Jacob said, 'Surely the LORD is in this place; and I knew it
not.' And he was afraid, and said, 'How dreadful is this place! This
is none other but the house of God, and this is the gate of heaven'"
(Genesis 28:16–17). We too can become as Jacob, caught up in our
wrongs and miss seeing God or knowing he is with us. Our issues
can distract us from God, thus, not knowing he is in the midst of us
and the situation.

God sends messages to us via dreams and visions; and in our
struggles, he speaks to us. If we could stand still for a moment,
breathe, do the three R's—relax, relate, release—we will see God
over the circumstance and see him and hear what he has to say to
us about our problem that is too great for us to figure out anyway.
Psalm 46:10 (KJV) instructs us, "'Be still, and know that I am God:
I will be exalted among the heathen; I will be exalted in the earth.
The LORD of host is with us; the God of Jacob is our refuge.' Selah."

Selah is known as a musical term. So worship God, give him
praise in the midst of it all, and eventually things will begin to turn
around for the good and you will gain a different perspective about
your situation.

There were many instances that I heard God speak to me, and I am sure the same goes for you. A recent occurrence is December 3, 2017. I stopped to get gas at Kroger, and as I walked back to my car to pump gas in the tank, a woman from church pulled up. I did not recognize her at first, but when she pulled up to the pump and rolled down her window, God spoke to my spirit softly but loudly saying, "Pay for her gas." And he said it a second time while we talked.

After we finished talking, I went to my car and pumped gas in my car tank, and he said it a third time, "Pay for her gas." So when she got out of her car, I called her name and said, "God told me to pay for your gas, and I want to be obedient." I remember saying to God when I got in my car after paying for her gas, "It is your money anyway." I realized as if realizing it for the first time that my money is his money. I told God, "We are in it together" (my saying to him quite often). As I shared my response with you about what I said to God that Sunday at the gas pump, I think my response was somewhat sarcastic, and I am smiling and thinking how much he loves me. (He did not smack me down!)

Another recent occurrence of hearing God speak to me was the day that a woman I know who's in her seventies had her book signing at Collinsville Public Library. This particular Saturday, November 25, 2017, I was thinking that the book signing was from 1:00 p.m. to 4:00 p.m. While I was getting dressed, I could hear this woman's voice talking loud in my right ear. It was if I could hear her conversation with the people in attendance at the book signing. I could not piece the conversation together, but I heard her voice loud and clear in my right ear. It was 12:50 p.m. when I left my house contemplating whether to go to the ATM to get money for the book purchase and money to pay for getting my car wash. My intentions was to get my car washed first. I remember thinking I would have time to get my car washed and then make it to the book signing because it would end at 4:00 p.m.

As soon as I got in my car and drove to the bottom of the hill, I decided to go to the book signing first since I could get there less than fifteen minutes. My thought was, *I'd stay for a short while and still have time to get my car washed.* When I turn onto the main road, her voice I was hearing stopped.

When I got to Collinsville Library, a librarian escorted me to the meeting room where the book signing was happening. I shared with those there what I planned to do before coming to the book signing and the time that I thought the book signing was occurring. The woman of the hour said, "It was from eleven o'clock to one."

I said, "I need to go to the bank to get cash to pay for the book and to get my car washed."

She said, "I am shutting everything down at one thirty."

Then I said to her, "Now I know why I kept hearing you talking in my ear, and it had to be God's way of telling me to go to the book signing first." I am glad that I *listened!* God knew my heart's desire was to support her and celebrate her achievement. So had I not *listened* to him, I would have missed being a part of her book-signing event.

Likewise, if Samuel had not *listened* to God, he would missed on anointing Saul as captain over God's people, Israel.

> Now the LORD had told Samuel in his ear a day before Saul came, saying, "To morrow [tomorrow] about this time I will send thee a man out of the land of Benjamin, and thou shalt anoint him to be captain over my people Israel, that he may save my people out of the land of the Philistines: for I have looked upon my people, because their cry is come unto me." (1 Samuel 9:15–16, KJV)

Notice God spoke to Samuel in his ear just as he spoke to me in my right ear. However, it was not God's voice per se as it was when he spoke to Samuel, but he transferred his voice through a voice that I would recognize. And because of this, I did not miss the book signing.

# CHAPTER 7

# God's Angels

> The LORD hath prepared his throne in the heavens; and his kingdom ruleth over all. Bless the LORD, ye his angels, that excel in strength, that do his commandments, hearkening unto the voice of his word. Bless ye the LORD, all ye his hosts; ye ministers of his, that do his pleasure. Bless the LORD, all his works in all places of his dominion: bless the LORD, O my soul. (Psalm 103:19–22, KJV)

This Psalm of David expresses his perception of how he saw the angels of God and how they are in position ready to act on the Word of God. Consider these few questions to ask yourself. How often are you *releasing* the Word of God into the atmosphere? Do you realize the *authority* in the Word of God? Have you *realized* the angels wait for us to release the Word of God so they can go to work in our behalf? This psalm lets us know that God has dominion over all, and the angels are subject to his Word.

Moreover, the Word of God informs us to be aware of our actions toward others because we could be entertaining an angel unaware. "Be not forgetful to entertain strangers: for thereby some have entertained angels unawares" (Hebrews 12:2). I am remindful of an experience some years ago in Danville, Virginia. It was mid-1990 when I lived there a brief while. One evening after work, I went to Food Lion to get a few groceries. At the checkout line was a young African American male (brown-skin complexion) who looked to be in his early teens (fourteen or fifteen). He was dressed in a white dress shirt and had on dark brown slacks with a belt. His overall appearance was neat. His dark brown hair was a short afro neatly in place. A person in front of me, who paid her groceries, was having a conversation with the cashier as the cashier scanned my groceries. As the young boy bagged my groceries, I talked to him, and he looked up and smiled. When I looked away for a split second after he finished bagging my groceries, he disappeared.

I remember looking around as I stood in the checkout line to see where he went because it was just a split second that I looked away. I remember asking the cashier, "Where is the young boy who bagged my groceries?" The cashier seemed puzzled as if she did not know what I was asking. I paid for my groceries and left Food Lion wondering where the young boy could have gone in such a split second! Later I ruled it as an angel that I entertained unaware.

After that encounter, I returned a few times to Food Lion but never saw the young boy who bagged my groceries. Still to this day, I can vision that particular evening and see the young boy in my mind. I do wonder what could have been his purpose for being there and his connection to me. Maybe I am thinking too much into it and should leave it alone because it was a supernatural phenomenon and was unexplainable.

Well, *God's angels* are spiritual beings that I believe can take on many shapes and forms. They are, of course, higher than humanity. "What is man, that thou art mindful of him and the son of man, that thou visitest him? For thou hast made him a little lower than the angels, and hast crowned him with glory and honour" (Psalm 8:4–5).

God created angels for his service and worship, and people are not to worship them. In the book of Revelation, John's experience of praising an angel lets us know that angels are not to be praise!

> And I John saw these things, and heard them.
> And when I had heard and seen, I fell down
> to worship before the feet of the angel which
> showed me these things. Then saith he unto me,
> "See thou do it not: for I am thy fellow servant,
> and of thy brethren the prophets, and of them
> which keep the sayings of this book: worship
> God." (Revelation 22:8–9)

*God's angels* are obedient to his commands. They disperse as God gives them order. Since God is the supreme ruler, and the only eternal and all-wise God, angels do as instructed. The believers of Christ Jesus have access to these angels and, by walking in God's authority, can pray to God or request him to summons them to places, to hold us up (keep you and me from falling), or combat at all hurt, harm, and danger.

> There shall no evil befall thee, neither shall any
> plague come nigh thy dwelling. For he shall give
> his angels charge over thee, to keep thee in all
> thy ways. They shall bear thee up in their hands,
> lest thou dash thy foot against a stone. (Psalm
> 91:10–12, KJV)

When the three Hebrews, Shadrach, Meshach, and Abednego were thrown into the fiery furnace because of refusing to bow to the golden image King Nebuchadnezzar erected, they did not command the angels to their rescue. They believe God will rescue them and told Nebuchadnezzar that the God they serve is able to deliver them from the burning furnace and out of his hand (Daniel 3:17). A step further, they told Nebuchadnezzar that if their God did not (deliver), they will not serve his gods nor worship the golden image (Daniel 3:18). Their belief in God and dedication to him moved him to send an angel to deliver them.

There other instances during biblical times where the believers of Christ delivered not because they command the angels but because God sent them. Refer to some of these examples: Daniel in the Lion's den (Daniel 6:22), Peter in prison (Acts 12:5; Acts 12:11), and the Israelites in Egypt (Numbers 20:16). As indicated, the angels hearken to God's Word, as well as to the voice of God's Word because this is their function as angels.

Remember, human beings were made a little lower than the angels were. So how is it that we can command them? We do not control the angels. Only God does for he created them. God did not create the angels to be everywhere at one time. Only God has the power to do this. "'Can any hide himself in secret places that I shall not see him?' saith the LORD. 'Do not I fill heaven and earth?' saith the LORD?" (Jeremiah 23:24, KJV). Angels do not know everything as we, human beings, do not know everything. Once again, God created the angels and us not to know all things. For instance, neither man nor angels know when Christ will return. According to the words of Jesus Christ, "But of that day and hour knoweth no man, no, not the angels of heaven, but my Father only" (Mark 13:32, KJV).

I indicated that angels listen to the voice of God's Word. I specified we release them through speaking God's Word and praying or requesting God to release them. However, you might debate the Word of God informs that we can bind and loose things on earth and in heaven. In the book of Matthew, Jesus Christ had a conversation with his disciples asking, "Whom do men say that I the Son of man am" (Matthew 16:13, KJV)?

The disciples answered reporting what some say he is (Matthew 16:14), but in Verse 15, Jesus says to them, "But whom say ye that I am" (Matthew 16:15, KJV)?

"Simon Peter spoke out and said, 'Thou art the Christ, the Son of the living God'" (Matthew 16:16, KJV).

> Jesus answered Peter and said, "Blessed art thou, Simon Barjona: for flesh and blood hath not revealed it unto thee, but my Father which is in heaven. And I say also unto thee, that thou art Peter, and upon this rock I will build my church;

and the gates of hell shall not prevail against it. And I will give unto thee the keys of the kingdom of heaven: and whatsoever thou shalt bind on earth shall be bound in heaven: and whatsoever thou shalt loose on earth shall be loosed in heaven." (Matthew 16:17–19, KJV)

Nevertheless, for such authority to occur that Jesus gave unto Peter, it has to come heavenward. In order for you and me to practice that same authority, it must come from God. He reveals to us what to bind and loose on earth and in heaven as we commune with him in prayer and spend time in his Word concerning a matter. The kingdom keys of heaven, in my perspective, are obtained through relationship with Christ, and his authority exercises through us. So when we quote the Scriptures, that is how those angels go to working, binding and loosing those things for us that we speak.

*God's angels* are heavenly beings, and through hearing the voice of God's Word, they take charge and do whatever they are commanded. The words of Jesus Christ:

Again I say unto you, "That if two of you shall agree on earth as touching any thing [anything] that they shall ask, it shall be done for them of my Father which is in heaven. For where two or three are gathered together in my name, there am I in the midst of them." (Matthew 18:19–20, KJV)

The angels of God have no choice but to act! It is good and perfectly all right if you arrive at another perspective regarding how things on earth and in heaven are bind and loose. The whole purpose is for you to search, discover, and arrive at what you believe God shows you. As I, we are learning and growing in this race. And with an open mind, we can learn together.

There are specific angels of God working around the clock. They act as guards to guard the eastside of the Garden of Eden as indicated in Genesis Chapter 3. "So he drove out the man; and he placed at the east of the garden of Eden Cherubims, and a flaming sword which turned every way, to keep the way of the tree of life" (Genesis 3:24, KJV). Adam commanded not to eat from the Tree of Knowledge of Good and Evil before the LORD acknowledge that it was not good for man to be alone (Genesis 2:16–17). Adam and his wife, Eve, disobeyed the command and did eat (Genesis 3:6). I often think that cherubims have the duty of keeping Adam and Eve out of the east of the Garden of Eden with a flaming sword turned in every angle to guard the Tree of Life. I know God can assign angels with flaming swords to guard my love ones, those connected to me, and me constantly (never ending). Since *God's angels* are ministering angels too, I believe they can forewarn us not to go here or there, and if we chose not to listen, we could end up in a pickle and reap the consequences. For an example, if we are distracted by our emotions and hell-bent on going or doing what we so desire (our flesh cravings) knowing internally we should not, there is a price to pay.

Another example is a biblical one. Balaam was ordered by God not to go to see Balak, for God knew what Balak wanted him to do, which was to curse God's people, Israel. Balaam was caught up in Balak giving him a house full of silver and gold and promoting him to great honor. He could not see that going with Balak's servants to Balak's house was a sin. Balaam knew he could not do less or more than God allowed, so he requested from Balak to tarry for the night before coming to him. Balaam let Balak know that by tarrying overnight, he could hear more of what the Lord would say unto him. God did come to him that night giving instructions that if the men (Balak's servants) come calling him, he is to rise up and go with them and do what he (God) say to do. Balaam did rise early, saddled his donkey, and went with Balak's servants of Moab. And God was not pleased that his anger burned against Balaam.

While on the journey to Balak's palace, the Lord sent an angel to stand in the way as opposition against him, and two servants were with Balaam. The donkey saw the angel of the Lord standing in the way with sword in hand drawn, so the donkey turned and went into the field. Balaam, furious with the donkey, smote it and turned it in the way toward the angel who he did not see. The donkey saw the angel with the drawn sword that he ran into the wall and crushed Balaam's foot, and Balaam struck the donkey again. Balaam struck the donkey a third time after the donkey fell down under Balaam, and the Lord opened the donkey's mouth, and the donkey spoke asking Balaam, "What have I done unto thee that you smite me three times?"

Of course, Balaam and the donkey have a conversation, and afterwards, the Lord opened Balaam's eyes to see the angel with drawn sword in his hand standing in the way (see Numbers chapter 22 for this amazing story). Last but not the least, if we are not careful and become occupied on what we see as best and think that God is in it, we could fail to see the danger ahead. We could miss God's warning and ignore his angels sent to help us.

## CHAPTER 8

# *Fallen Angels*

As indicated in Chapter 7, God's angels created were by him. He created the fallen angels as well. Nevertheless, what is different about the *fallen angels* versus God's angels is that Satan influenced these angels. Let me briefly explain what I mean about the *fallen angels* influenced by Satan.

You see, Satan is also known as Lucifer as well as many other names viewed as attractive and stunning. The reason for this thought surfaced from the words God spoke through the prophet Ezekiel. In the book of Ezekiel, Satan is described as "full of wisdom and perfect in beauty" (Ezekiel 28:12).

> Thou (Satan) hast been in the Garden of Eden and every precious stone was thy covering; the sardius, topaz, and the diamond, the beryl, the onyx, and the jasper, the sapphire, the emerald, and the carbuncle, and gold: the workmanship of thy tabrets and of thy pipes was prepared in thee in the day that thou wast created. (Ezekiel 28:13)

Ezekiel articulated Satan as the "anointed cherub that covereth, thou wast upon the holy mountain of God and hast walked up and down in the midst of the stones of fire" (Ezekiel 28:14). Ezekiel specified Satan as "perfect in thy ways from the day that thou wast created, till iniquity was found in thee" (Ezekiel 28:15).

In addition, Satan was removed from his heavenly post due to the iniquity in him.

> How art thou fallen from heaven, O Lucifer, son of the morning! How art thou cut down to the ground, which didst weaken the nations? For thou hast said in thy heart, "I will ascend into heaven, I will exalt my throne above the stars of God: I will sit also upon the mount of the congregation, in the sides of the north: I will ascend above the heights of the clouds; I will be like the most High" (referring to God). Yet thou shalt be brought down to hell, to the sides of the pit [abyss]. (Isaiah 14:12–15, KJV)

Satan, in his pride and false glory, influenced a third of the angelic host to band with him against the one and only Most High God, the true and living God, the everlasting Father, the Prince of Peace, the bright and morning Star, and God Eternal.

> And his tail drew the third part of the stars of heaven, and did cast them to the earth: and the dragon stood before the woman which was ready to be delivered, for to devour her child as soon as it was born. And the great dragon was cast out, that old serpent, called the Devil, and Satan, which deceiveth the whole world: he was cast out into the earth, and his angels were cast out with him. (Revelation 12:4,9, KJV).

Before Satan was cast out of heaven, his appearance had already changed. His stunning and attractive form had lost its appeal. As indicated in Revelation 12:9, his appearance was that of a dragon. Revelation 12:7–8 (KJV) says, "And there was a war in heaven:

Michael and his angels fought against the dragon; and the dragon fought and his angels. And prevailed not; neither was their place found any more in heaven."

Satan and his angels lost citizenship in heaven, and that is why he is an accuser of the brethren and roaming the earth to wreak havoc because his time is short (wants you, everyone, and me to fall prey to him and not gain eternal life).

> Then I heard a loud voice saying in heaven, "Now is come salvation, and strength, and the kingdom of our God, and the power of his Christ: for the accuser of our brethren is cast down, which accused them before our God day and night.
> "Therefore rejoice, ye heavens, and ye that dwell in them. Woe to the inhabiters of the earth and of the sea! for the devil is come down unto you, having great wrath, because he knoweth that he hath but a short time." (Revelation 12:10,12)

Accordingly, as God has his angels to do his bidden, Satan has his demons (a third of the angelic host) to do his propositions too! The Bible lets us know that Jesus reveals Satan as a murderer from the beginning and the truth is not in him.

> Ye are of your father the devil, and the lusts of your father ye will do. He was a murderer from the beginning, and abode not in the truth, because there is no truth in him. When he speaketh a lie, he speaketh of his own: for he is a liar, and the father of it. (John 8:44, KJV)

Humanity may wonder why such evil has corrupted the world and hatred, racism, bigotry, and self-glory are spread throughout the earth.

Scripture John 8:44 is an evident answer to the turmoil we see occurring on earth from people who yield to Satan's lies and deceptions. Satan is not about love. He has always been about his own motives, and as indicated in this chapter, he desired to dethrone God (Isaiah 14:13). The devil wanted to be like God (Isaiah 14:14). God is love and always have us (the world) in mind. "For God so loved the world, that he gave his only begotten Son, that whosoever believeth in him should not perish, but have everlasting life" (John 3:16, KJV).

"'For I know the thoughts that I think toward you,' saith the LORD, 'thoughts of peace, and not evil, to give you an expected end'" (Jeremiah 29:11, KJV).

What a beautiful world we could be in if the love of Christ rests in the hearts of the evildoers. All the evildoers need to do is yield to the love of Christ, receive and accept him as their savior, and live a life pleasing to God. Satan is not their friend nor cares about their soul. Satan is doomed for everlasting damnation. His end is fire and brimstone. Never will he see rest and have peace. He and his followers are destined for the same destruction and torment. And the devil that deceived them was cast into the lake of fire and brimstone, where the beast and the false prophet are, and shall be tormented day and night for ever and ever (Revelation 20:10).

I can remember two instances propositioned by Satan while praying to God about my financial difficulties. He presented to me through his whispers, "If you bow down to me, I will give you the world." Why was his proposal not strange to me? Why did I not bow and allow him to show me his offers? Why did I not become a victim to his enticing words?

The answers to each question are simple and plain. First I sold out to God! I know he would never leave nor forsake me. The words of Jesus Christ, "...lo, I am with you always, even unto the end of the world" (Matthew 28:20, KJV). Secondly Satan tempted Jesus with the same proposition.

In the Gospel of Matthew, Matthew indicates three instances where Satan tempted Jesus. "Then was Jesus led up of the Spirit into the wilderness to be tempted of the devil" (Matthew 4:1, KJV). "And when he had fasted forty days and forty nights, he was afterward an hungered" (Matthew 4:2).

Temptation 1:

> "And when the tempter [devil] came to him, he said, 'If thou be the Son of God, command that these stones be made bread'" (Matthew 4:3).

Temptation 2:

> Then the devil taketh him up into the holy city, and setteth him on a pinnacle of the temple. And saith unto him, 'If thou be the Son of God, cast thyself down: for it is written, He shall give his angels charge concerning thee: lest at any time thou dash thy foot against a stone.' (Matthew 4:5–6)

Temptation 3:

> Again, the devil taketh him up unto an exceeding high mountain, and showeth him all the kingdoms of the world, and the glory of them; And saith unto him, "All these things will I give thee, if thou wilt fall down and worship me." (Matthew 4:8–9, KJV)

Nevertheless, with each temptation Satan presented to Jesus, Jesus resisted. In temptation 1, Jesus lets Satan know in Matthew 4:4 (KJV) that "It is written, Man shall not live by bread alone, but by every word that proceedeth out of the mouth of God."

In temptation 2, Jesus tells Satan, "It is written again, 'Thou shalt not tempt the Lord thy God'" (Matthew 4:7). In temptation 3, Jesus responded to Satan, "Get thee hence, Satan: for it is written, Thou shalt worship the Lord thy God, and him only shalt thou serve" (Matthew 4:10).

In each temptation, Jesus made sure that Satan knew who he serves and reminded Satan that the Lord is God (his God too!) and he should serve and worship the Lord.

Like I have indicated, I remember those two times the devil approached me while praying to God about my finances, and boldly, I told him, "Get thee behind me, Satan. I do not belong to you. I belong to the Lord God Almighty. He is my God! He only will I bow down to and not you."

The devil failed to realize that he has no authority over Jesus Christ and no authority over me. Satan only has control over those who refuse Jesus Christ or have been allusion by his deceits that they fell victim to a *fallen angel*.

The devil presents as an angel of light and is deceiving many. 2 Corinthians 11:14 (KJV) specifies, "And no marvel; for Satan himself is transformed into an angel of light." Sadly, those who are sold out to Satan know it is hard to break away from his powers because they have allowed him to have dominion over them. Satan tricked them into falling for his lies and gave them a taste of what he could do and give them, so after he snared them, he revealed his true colors. In other words, Satan showed his true side—a deadly side.

The words of Jesus Christ in the Gospel of John mentions, "The thief cometh not, but for to steal, and to kill, and to destroy: I am come that they might have life, and that they might have it more abundantly" (John 10:10, KJV). You can denounce Satan and all his dark practices and live for Jesus Christ (receive Christ today).

# CHAPTER 9

# Redemption Part 1: Fall of Man

The earth is full of birth pains and is still giving birth to many devastating and catastrophic disasters. In the Gospel of Matthew, as specified in the KJV, Jesus answers his disciples' questions regarding a sign about his coming and the end of the world. And Jesus answered and said unto them:

> Take heed that no man deceive you. For many shall come in my name, saying I am Christ; and shall deceived many. And ye shall hear of wars and rumours of wars: see that ye be not troubled: for all these things must come to pass, but the end is not yet. For nation shall rise against nation, and kingdom against kingdom: and there shall be famines, and pestilences, and earthquakes, in divers places. All these are the beginning of sorrows [birth pains]. (Matthew 24:4–8)

Well, the fall of man occurred in the Garden of Eden. Adam and Eve disobeyed God, and through their disobedience, there came sorrow, death, and a change in humanity, the earth, and the atmosphere. When Adam and Eve ate from the forbidden tree, they became wise as their eyes opened and realized their nakedness. They hid among the trees in the garden when they heard the voice of God walking in the garden in the cool of day. In their conversation with God, Eve blamed the serpent, and Adam blamed his wife (Eve) for giving him the fruit from the tree in the middle of the garden, which he did eat (Genesis 3:1–13).

Adam, Eve, and the serpent received consequences for their actions. The book of Genesis informs that God cursed the serpent "above all cattle and above every beast of the field, and upon thy belly shall thou go [crawl] and dust shall thou eat all the days of thy life" (Genesis 3:14, KJV). God put enmity between the serpent and Eve and both their seed, informing them "it shall bruise thy head, and thou shalt bruise his heel" (Genesis 3:15, KJV). God said to Eve he will "greatly multiply thy sorrow and thy conception; in sorrow thou shalt bring forth children; and thy desire shall be to thy husband, and he shall rule over thee" (Genesis 3:16, KJV).

God issued penalties to Adam too. God declares:

> And unto Adam he said, "Because thou hast eaten of the tree, of which I commanded thee, saying, 'Thou shalt not eat of it: cursed is the ground for thy sake; in sorrow shalt thou eat of it all the days of thy life.' Thorns also and thistles shall it bring forth to thee; and thou shalt eat the herb of the field.
> "In the sweat of face shalt thou eat bread, till thou return unto the ground; for out of it wast thou taken: for dust thou art, and unto dust shalt thou return." (Genesis 3:17–19, KJV)

It is recorded in the book of Genesis about the first murder between man occurred. Adam and Eve had two sons named Cain and Abel. Cain kills Abel because God respected Abel's first fruit, which came from his flocks. Cain presented God with a fruit offering of the ground, and he was not pleased. And Cain became cruel in heart, and it showed on his face (Genesis 4:1–5).

A thought comes to mind: Do you think if Cain bought God a sacrifice that was not fruit of the ground but from Abel's flocks, his heart would had not grew vicious? Remember, Cain was a tiller of the ground and Abel, keeper of sheep (Genesis 4:2).

Do you think Abel would had showed Cain how to sacrifice a sheep for an offering to the Lord? I think Abel would have because of the significance of the sheep versus Cain tilling the ground. Adam came from the dust of the ground and will till it and will return to it (Genesis 2:7, 3:17, 19). Eve came from his rib (Genesis 2:21–22), and the serpent cursed to crawl on its belly and eat dust for the days of its life (Genesis 3:14). The ground was cursed, produced thorns and thistles (Genesis 3:18), so in order to get vegetation from it, it has to be tilled. In other words, the ground was hardened from the *fall of man,* and Cain's sacrifice was viewed as a representation of his stony and callous heart. A malice heart does not change overnight unless God does the miraculous. God asked Cain about his inner hatred and countenance, as well as told him he would be accepted if he does well, and the result of what happens when he does not do well; sin would rule over him (Genesis 4:6–7).

My perspective regarding the conversation between God and Cain is that Cain was receiving the best counseling about his current situation. He chose not to deal with his issue, and as a result, the sin that ruled him over powered him to the point that he acted out his venomous heart and killed his brother, Abel (Genesis 4:8). After Cain murdered his brother, his heart was prideful that he responded to God sarcastically when God asks him in Genesis 4:9 (KJV), "'Where is Abel, thy brother?' Cain answered, 'I know not: Am I my brother's keeper?'"

The biblical story of Cain and Abel clearly demonstrates good and evil, a conscious of doing what is right as opposed to doing what is wrong and hate against love. In today's world where there is demonstration of hate, racism, power, and control, no love, right is wrong and wrong is right, and self-motives, it is visible that a person struggling with a pride heart clings to gratifying his or her entice-ments or demons. I am sure Cain could focus on no one but himself. He could only see how his pride was tampered and feeling belittled about his incapability to do what was right that to boast in himself to get recognition is to carry out a crime.

A person with a Cain mentality will become a victim to Satan's deceptions every time. Instead of resisting Satan and submitting to God, the person rather carry out the giant that has taken control over his or her emotions, thoughts, and life. You would think what makes a person a bigger person is to admit what he or she is battling and get help. Confront the issue and get it under control. Why go through life as damaged good when you do not have to? Why damage another life because of recklessness about improving yourself? Take ownership of your flaws and fix them.

In the book of James, James specifies:

> But if ye have bitter envying and strife in your hearts, glory not, and lie not against the truth. This wisdom descendeth not from above, but is earthly, sensual, [and] devilish. For where envying and strife is, there is confusion and every evil work. (James 3:14–16, KJV)

James further informs, "But now ye rejoice in your boastings: all such rejoicing is evil. Therefore to him that knoweth to do good, and doeth it not, to him it is sin" (James 4:16–17). James suggests an encouraging solution, which is:

> Submit yourselves therefore to God. Resist the devil, and he will flee from you. Draw nigh to God, and he will draw nigh to you. Cleansed your hands, ye sinners; and purify your hearts, ye double minded. (James 4:7–8)

"A double minded man is unstable in all his ways" (James 1:8).

Moreover, the Cain and Abel story and the profound wisdom of James, which he indicates comes from above, causes me to reflect again on my brother losing his life at the hands of *Judas* who could be viewed as having had a Cain mentality. I have no idea of what he is like today, but I know what he was like when the incident occurred December 1996. How vividly the imprints of the orange jail jumpsuit *Judas* clothed in as the trial took place. He looked gravely intense as his head hung down, and not once did he look in the direction of my family and me or tell us he was sorrowful for what he had done. If he had expressed his sorrow, most likely, it would not register to my family and me because we were grief-stricken. And by the grace of God, I endured hearing about the instances that led up to the death of my brother. My mother could not take it! She burst out crying and had to be removed from the courtroom. My aunt and I sat staring as if we were in space somewhere.

You know, reflecting back on the trial, I was hurt, and it hurt like hell! Thoughts going through my mind of wanting to defend my brother when the defense attorney for *Judas* attempted to taint my deceased brother's character. I constantly thought, *How unfair because my brother is not here to defend himself.*

I felt violated as if I had no voice. My family had no voice. I thought about the night before *Judas* murdered my brother. He made Spencer get on his knees (told to my family) outside of Burger King (Collinsville, Virginia location) in the parking lot as he pointed the gun at Spencer's head. Then I thought about how *Judas* was surprisingly on foot, walked up to my brother who was at the first carwash stall helping the guys he was with clean one of the guys' girlfriend car. It was nighttime when the incident occurred. They were at the Exxon convenient store on Commonwealth Boulevard, and *Judas* shot Spencer in the chest using a 9mm gun. The Exxon convenient store is not in operation as of 2018. The gas pumps have been removed but the car wash is still in place and opened for public use.

Although the tragic occurred, the angel of God was on the scene. The angel of God prevented *Judas* from shooting my brother in the head at Burger King. Could you imagine what the 9mm shot would had done to my brother's head to his face? The shot to his chest caused an internal explosion to his vital organs (heart and lungs). The fallen angel was on the scene too and was most likely had been enticing *Judas* to kill my brother prior to him carrying out the act. I do not know the full gist of the entire story, but God knows and

*Judas* knows. Just like Cain, *Judas* did not face his demons, resist the devil, and acknowledge to himself his flaws and inward struggles. *Judas* chose to follow a heart of pride and confusion. He chose to put himself on display for bragging rights to a senseless and cruel crime. I do not know the validity of the report, but a family member of mine learned that *Judas* bragged about killing my brother to an inmate who thought highly of my family that the person gave him a beating that he would not forget.

One thing that I can fully conclude from this tragic is the peace of God has guarded my heart and pushed out the hurt. Bitterness and unforgiveness are not present in my heart, and why is this the case? I chose to allow God to take over the pain, bitterness, and unforgiveness. Since I opened my heart to God so he would have free reign to heal me, I am able to tell the story for my family and be at peace about it. I know the familiar saying goes that time heals all wounds, but it is a process. And while I was in the process, it took effort on my part to examine my own heart. It took *several* self-talk conversations about holding on or letting go of the hurt, bitterness, and unforgiveness that was trying to clutch me.

While in the process, I had to be true with my feelings and wrestle with my feelings constantly. I experienced several emotional rollercoaster rides before arriving at total restoration of peace. Confession to God about my thoughts and feelings had its challenging moments because guilt feelings tried to invade my moods, so there were times that I repressed the bitterness, hurt, or unforgiveness.

Guess what I learned about repressing bitterness, hurt, and unforgiveness? It returned to the surface of my heart, and I faced having to admit those emotions had not gone anywhere. I discovered to embrace guilt as part of the process, so I could look to God to help me get it out of my heart. I discovered that God still loved me and the guilt feelings were not from him but a trick from Satan to hold me as a bound hostage. Satan did not want me free because his plot toward me was to hinder the spiritual progress that God had begun in me. The devil wanted my life to turn upside down and become a wreck! When the Word of God says, "nothing shall pluck us out of his hand," better believe it! Nothing will! Satan operated through

*Judas* to throw a curve ball, but God already had the solution. He had me grounded and rooted in him. Jesus states plainly in the Gospel of John:

> My sheep hear my voice, and I know them, and they follow me: And I give unto them eternal life; and they shall never perish, neither shall any man pluck them out of my hand. My father, which gave them me [gave me him], is greater than all; and no man is able to pluck them [me] out of my Father's hand. I and my Father are one. (John 10:27–30, KJV)

In the midst of it all, God demonstrated his strength through me in the loss of my brother and the trial. God used me as a pillar to my family and showed me what he can do in and through me.

Lastly what makes the completely unfortunate situation unique, at the appointed time, God had me to cross path with *Judas's* defense attorney. I parked my car in the parking lot across from the City Post Office. And before getting out of my car, I noticed the defense attorney walking to his car. I politely said, "Excuse me but are you so and so who defended *Judas* in the murder case of Spencer Moyer?"

He said *yes* with a smirk look, as if he had succeeded in defending *Judas*. I indicated in Chapter 1 that *Judas* got five years for killing my brother, but I rejoiced because the verdict was guilty; and my heart's desire was for the jury to find *Judas* guilty. I proceeded to say in a calm voice as I look him directly in his eyes saying, "The person murdered was my brother." His smirk look disappeared suddenly, and he said "I am sorry" as he walked away.

I remained in my car, watched him get into his car, and he drove off. I had to regroup before getting out of my car because it had been a few months since the trial ended. The hurt I felt was still fresh. The debate to let go or continue to hold on to the hurt was still processing. I knew God gave me strength and a calmness to approach the attorney. It felt surreal, and all I could say in a whispered voice while gazing, "God, I know it was you."

God can change a corrupt heart to peace, love, and honesty. So give him a chance. Make him your choice. Learn of him and get to know his wonderful love.

# CHAPTER 10

# Redemption Part 2: Ultimate Sacrifice

As mentioned in chapter 9, man fell through disobedience and tapped into curiosity presented to him by the serpent. The woman beguiled by the serpent that she ate from the forbidden tree, and turned and coax her husband (Adam) to eat from the tree, which God had commanded them not to eat of it, touch it, lest they die (see Genesis 3:3).

Because of the fall of man, God issued consequences to Adam, Eve, and the serpent. Out of Adam and Eve's union, Cain and Abel were born through sorrow (Genesis 3:16). Cain ended up slewing Abel out of jealousy because God did not respect him neither his offering (Genesis 4:5,8). Thorns and thistles were produced from the cursed ground (Genesis 3:18). The serpent was cursed above all cattle and beast of the field, and put on its belly to crawl and eat dust for the rest of its days in life (Genesis 3:14). God put animosity between Eve and the serpent, her seed and its seed. The seed from Eve and the serpent: "it shall bruise thy head, and thou shalt bruise his heel" (Genesis 3:15, KJV).

Since the fall of man, the first Adam brought forth sin in the world; God had a solution to save humankind. A second Adam had to come on the scene, which lead to a remarkable and a turning point for humanity. The prophet Isaiah foretold the birth of Jesus Christ. "Therefore the Lord himself shall give you a sign; Behold, a virgin shall conceive, and bear a son, and shall call his name Immanuel" (Isaiah 7:14, KJV).

The Gospel of Matthew verifies Isaiah's prophecy by announcing:

> Now the birth of Jesus Christ was on this wise: When as his mother Mary was espoused to Joseph, before they came together, she was found with child of the Holy Ghost. Then Joseph her husband, being a just man, and not willing to make her a public example, was minded to put her away privily. But while he thought on these things, behold, the angel of the Lord appeared unto him in a dream, saying, "Joseph, thou son of David, fear not to take unto thee Mary thy wife: for that which is conceived in her is of the Holy Ghost. And she shall bring forth a son, and thou shalt call his name JESUS: for he shall save his people from their sins." Now all this was done, that it might be fulfilled which was spoken of the Lord by the prophet, saying, "Behold, a virgin shall be with child, and shall bring forth a son, and they shall call his name Emmanuel" (which, being interpreted, is God with us). (Matthew 1:18–23, KJV)

Jesus, according to God's perfect plan, exchanged his heavenly attire for a temporary earthly apparel. But made himself of no reputation, and took upon him the form of a servant, and was made in the likeness of men: "And being found in fashion as a man, he humbled himself, and became obedient unto death, even the death of the cross" (Philippians 2:7–8, KJV).

Since Adam failed humanity through sinning, humanity needed restoration. The second Adam (Jesus Christ) who was without sin became the scapegoat to carry out redemption. Hebrews 4:15 (KJV), "For we have not an high priest which cannot be touched with the feeling of our infirmities; but was in all points tempted like as we are, yet without sin."

Jesus became the blood sacrifice for humanity. He was faultless and had not filtered sin into man. In other words, Jesus did no wrong! The love of his Father made Adam wrong right by sending him (Jesus) into a depraved world to save the world. Not only did Isaiah prophesied Jesus's coming into the world through the virgin Mary, but also, he would be a sin offering.

> Yet it pleased the LORD to bruise him; he hath put him to grief: when thou shalt make his soul an offering for sin, he shall see his seed, he shall prolong his days, and the pleasure of the LORD shall prosper in his hand. (Isaiah 53:10, KJV)

Furthermore, Jesus, the scapegoat for us and is the Lamb of God, took on slaughtering clothing for you and me to not only demonstrate obedience to the Father but to demonstrate unconditional love that he has for us. Isaiah prophesied, "He was oppressed, and he was afflicted, yet he opened not his mouth: he is brought as a lamb to the slaughter, and as a sheep before her shearers is dumb, so he openeth not his mouth" (Isaiah 53:7). Like I've always heard in church about Jesus from a child to an adult, "He never said a mumbling word."

Jesus knew his hour had come, for the Gospel of Mark informs:

> And he taketh with him Peter and James and John, and began to be sore amazed, and to be very heavy; and saith unto them, "My soul is exceeding sorrowful unto death: tarry ye here, and watch." And he went forward a little, and fell on the ground, and prayed that, if it were possible, the hour might pass from him. (Mark 14:33–35, KJV)

Jesus Christ, the son of the living God, was obedient even unto death although he did ask the Father to "take away this cup (facing harsh punishment leading to death on the cross) from me."

"And he said, 'Abba, Father, all things are possible unto thee; take away this cup from me: nevertheless not what I will, but what thou wilt'" (Mark 14:36). Jesus was arrested and was led to the high priest.

> And they led Jesus away to the high priest: and with him were assembled all the chief priests and the elders and the scribes. And the chief priests and all the council sought for witness against Jesus to put him to death; and found none. For many bare false witness against him, but their witness agreed not together. (Mark 14:53, 55–56, KJV)

Mark 14:65 (KJV) says, "And some began to spit on him, and to cover his face, and to buffet him, and to say unto him, 'Prophesy: and the servants did strike him with the palms of their hands.'"

Jesus was delivered into the hands of Pilate who found no fault in him, exchanged for the murderer (Barabbas) release, and he faced crucifixion at the cries of the people (Mark 15:1–15). When the third hour approached, Jesus was crucified. "And it was the third hour, and they crucified him" (Mark 15:25).

Darkness came over the whole land when it was the sixth hour and remained until the ninth hour. At the ninth hour, Jesus cried with a loud voice feeling forsaken and gave up the Ghost (he died) (Mark 15:33, 34, and 37). Isaiah prophesied that "he [Jesus] made his grave with the wicked, and with the rich in his death; because he had done no violence, neither was any deceit in his mouth" (Isaiah 53:9).

Moreover, when Jesus died, the veil in the temple ripped top to bottom. A confirmation is Mark 15:38 (KJV), "And the veil of the temple was rent in twain from top to the bottom." Jesus did rise from the dead and "appeared first before Mary Magdalene" then "unto two of them" and "afterward appeared unto the eleven" (disciples) before ascending to "sat on the right hand of God" (Mark 16:9, 12, 14 and 19).

Because of Jesus sacrificing his life for you and me, we have access to the Father. We can approach the throne of God boldly and make our request known unto him. Hebrews 4:16 (KJV), "Let us therefore come boldly unto the throne of grace, that we may obtain mercy, and find grace to help in time of need."

Jesus Christ has become our intercessor or mediator for Hebrews 9:15 (KJV) indicates:

> And for this cause he is the mediator of the new testament, that by means of death, for the redemption of the transgressions that were under the first testament, they which are called might receive the promise of eternal inheritance.

Hebrews 9:24 (KJV) states, "For Christ is not entered into the holy places made with hands, which are the figures of the true; but into heaven itself, now to appear in the presence of God for us."

The sacrificing of bulls and goats are obsolete, for Christ came as the high priest in which he is the *perfect tabernacle* who had not spots or blemishes to be offer up as a blood sacrifice. Hebrews 9:11–14 (KJV) points out:

> But Christ being come an high priest of good things to come, by a greater and more perfect tabernacle, not made with hands, that is to say, not of this building: Neither by the blood of goats and calves, but by his own blood he entered in once into the holy place, having obtained eternal redemption for us. For if the blood of bulls and of goats, and the ashes of an heifer sprinkling the unclean, sanctifieth to the purifying of the flesh: How much more shall the blood of Christ, who through the eternal Spirit offered himself with-

out spot to God, purge your conscience from dead works to serve the living God?

The giving up of his (Jesus Christ) life for us to have abundant life and life eternal is remarkable; better yet, there is no word to describe what Christ did for us. In the Gospel of John, Christ tells the Pharisees:

> The thief cometh not, but for to steal, and to kill, and to destroy: I am come that they [you and me] might have life, and that they (you and me) might have it more abundantly. I am the good shepherd: the good shepherd giveth his life for the sheep [us]. (John 10:10–11, KJV)

What a victorious life one could have in Jesus if only he or she would surrender.

> For he is our God; and we are the people of his pasture, and the sheep of his hand. To day [today] if ye will hear his voice, harden not your heart, as in the provocation and as in the day of temptation in the wilderness: When your fathers tempted me, proved me, and saw my work.
> Be not as the stubborn Israelites were when they wander in the wilderness. Forty years long was I grieved with this generation, and said, "It is a people that do err in their heart, and they have not known my ways." (Psalm 95:7–10, KJV)

Hebrews 3:15 (KJV) says, "While it is said, 'To day [today] if ye will hear his voice, harden not your hearts, as in the provocation.'" In other words, get rid of your disbelief and believe that Jesus Christ is the son of the living God and he does exist. He is the chief cornerstone that the builders rejected (Ephesians 2:20; Psalm 118:22; Matthew 21:42).

Jesus is the head of the church, the foundation that holds us together. Without him, we can do nothing, but with him, we can do all things. The Gospel of John 15:5 (KJV) says when Jesus talks about the vine and the branches: "I am the vine, ye are the branches: He that abideth in me, and I in him, the same bringeth forth much fruit: for without me ye can do nothing."

In the book of Philippians, Paul's letter to the Philippians indicates, "I can do all things through Christ which strengtheneth me" (Philippians 4:13). So you see, in Christ, we can do all things!

As I see it and is a living witness, Jesus Christ is our substance and lifeline. He is the lifter of our heads and the remover of all guilt and shame. He is the solid rock of ages, bread of life, keeper and sustainer, protector and provider, and salvation. And he will never leave you. He only is my "rock and my salvation: he is my defense; I shall not be moved. In God is my salvation and my glory: the rock of my strength, and my refuge, is in God" (Psalm 62:6–7, KJV).

He is God who is full of compassion and forgives our faults. He does not remind us of our wrongs but erase them forevermore. "I, even I, am he that blotteth out thy transgressions for mine own sake, and will not remember thy sins" (Isaiah 43:25, KJV). "For I will be merciful to their unrighteousness, and their sins and their iniquities will I remember no more" (Hebrews 8:12).

God desires the best for us, and it pleases him to give us the best. "And God is able to make all grace abound toward you that ye, always having all sufficiency in all things, may abound to every good work" (2 Corinthians 9:8, KJV).

James 1:17 (KJV) enlightens, "Every good gift and every perfect gift is from above, and cometh down from the Father of lights, with whom is no variableness, neither shadow of turning."

"But my God shall supply all your need according to his riches in glory by Christ Jesus" (Philippians 4:19, KJV).

"Let them shout for joy, and be glad, that favour my righteous cause: yea, let them say continually, Let the LORD be magnified, which hath pleasure in the prosperity of his servant" (Psalm 35:27, KJV). "The LORD taketh pleasure in them that fear him, in those that hope in his mercy" (Psalm 147:11).

One of my favorite Scriptures is Deuteronomy 8:18 (KJV) which states, "But thou shalt remember the LORD thy God: for it is he that giveth thee power to get wealth, that he may establish his covenant which he swore unto thy fathers, as it is this day."

I perceive this Scripture saying to me that God will show how to obtain wealth and prosper continuously. He will give the tools needed to prosper. He will connect me to those who are prospering to mentor me because he will give them spiritual eyes to see the potential in me and how to assist in bringing it out of me. Likewise, I will do the same—help others as I am helped. I am fully aware not to make a god out of wealth but to honor God with my substance as he gives it. Now this does not mean that I wait for the wealth to unfold but give him my substance by planting seeds (money) in church, those he lays on my heart, to an organization or scholarship fund. In other words, give to others. Do not close your hand; open it! Refer to Deuteronomy 15:7–8 about not shutting up your hand. Instead, open your hand wide.

Additionally, in the book of Deuteronomy 8:19 (KJV), it instructs, "And it shall be, if thou do at all forget the LORD thy God, and walk after other gods, and serve them, and worship them, I testify against you this day that ye shall surely perish."

God is a jealous God, and he does not want us to have any other gods before him. Exodus 34:14 (KJV) implies, "For thou shalt worship no other god: for the LORD, whose name is jealous, is a jealous God." And 1Corinthians 10:22 (KJV) asks, "Do we provoke the Lord to jealousy? Are we stronger than he?"

"Our arm is too short to box with God," James Weldon Johnson said.

# CHAPTER 11

# *Challenging Decisions*

Well, I think I am ready to end my story, but before I do, it is imperative that I reveal another life experience. Truthfully, I have two more life experiences to share. I can recall the first time that I learned that I had fibrocystic breast while residing in the Norfolk, Virginia, area.

In my mid-twenties, I did a breast examination because of noticing pain in my breasts as I walked up and down the stairs. It seemed that at any time when there was movement such as running, stretching, or going up and down the steps, my breasts ached. The pain occurred before my menstrual cycle, and this had been happening for about three months. I ruled it to be my body going through changes because it is a normal occurrence before my cycle started, and when that happens, my body goes through different variations (bloating, breasts tenderness, and cramping). However, this time, these body changes, or shall I say breasts changes, were consistent regarding how my breasts felt. And the breast pains felt the same.

Nevertheless, I noticed the knots in my breasts did not go away. I felt knots in both breast whenever I did the self-breast examination. You know, I did those breast examinations more than once each day until I went to see a doctor. I did the breast exam in the shower and out of the shower and before I went to bed and mornings before showering. I guess I was hoping it (knots) would go away and the pain. After contemplating about keeping my doctor appointment or not because of thinking the worst, I went anyway, and the doctor referred me to a surgeon for further examination. I decided to pray about what was happening to my breasts and no longer own the responsibility of what could be since I knew it was out of my hand. I needed God to step in and take the condition that was beyond my control. I remember praying, "Father, when I go see the surgeon, let him tell me I do not need surgery."

Appointment time with the surgeon! I dressed in the examination gown given to me by the nurse and put it on as instructed—make sure this side faces the front (opening of the gown). I sat patiently on the examining table waiting to see the surgeon and prayed while I waited. Finally the surgeon came in and examined my breasts, and he said, "You do not need surgery. You have a lumpy breast. If you can live with having a lumpy breast, you will be fine."

I smiled with a *big* smile and said *really*.

He said *yes*. My response was, "Thank God!" Then, of course, I started asking a ton of questions. I wanted to know what causes lumps to form in the breast, what I could do to alleviate the pain, and what the medical terminology for the diagnosis was. He told me the medical terminology is fibrocystic breast.

He discussed with me about changing my diet and gave me a handout that informed the type of foods and drinks to avoid. As I glanced at the handout, I saw two things that caught my eyes, and those were tea and chocolate. He mentioned caffeine and chocolate are not good for me. Chocolate has caffeine in it. I responded, "I do not drink coffee, but I love to drink hot tea and love me some chocolates."

He said, "Give up the caffeine." He mentioned to stay away from soft drinks and teas containing caffeine. We talked about red meats and vitamins such as vitamin C, E, and B6. The vitamins indicated were good deterrents to relieving fibrocystic symptoms. I recollect leaving the doctor's appointment feeling good and educated and glad to have the handout, as well as I researched more about the disease.

I remember becoming selective in the teas and soft drinks that I consumed. I start to drink more water too and love it! It was not hard for me to give up caffeine tea and soft drinks and gradually cut back on chocolates. After a while (few months), I started to notice the breasts pain subsiding, but the lumps remained. As of now, I have no breast pain, but the lumpy breasts remain.

I continue to do breast exams but not frequently as I did when I initially encountered the problem. I continue to drink plenty of water. I do not drink anything with caffeine. I drink decaffeinated tea and soft drink (usually a ginger ale or light color soda like Sprite or Cierra Mist when needing to get a good ole belch).

Now occasionally, I will drink hot chocolate during the cold months (in moderation). I do eat chocolate sometimes, but I try to eat dark chocolate. And if not, I eat milk chocolate, but this is not frequently. Sometimes, I admit I get on a chocolate kick, and if I buy a king-sized chocolate candy bar, I eat the whole candy bar. And if I buy ice cream, it has to have chocolate in it, and I may eat a big bowl full. As a result, one of my breasts ache slightly, so I leave it alone for a while. The same occurs when I drink more than one cup of hot chocolate. I must say that since becoming proactive and doing my best to take care of my body, I noticed no pain in my breasts. Praying and speaking to my body telling it to align with the Word of God; by Jesus stripes you are healed (Isaiah 53:5). I have not had any issues with my breasts so far. I pray God continue to have mercy on me, and it stays that way: no breasts concerns or other critical medical issues.

The breasts problems occurred in the late 1980s; however, in early 1990s up to 2005, another medical condition occurred. Let me tell you about the medical condition I once had. Notice I said "I once had." The condition robbed me of having children. The ailment forced me into a position whereas I had to make *challenging decisions*. Oftentimes, the illness caused me to think about the woman with an issue of blood (Matthew 9:20–22; Luke 8:43–48; Mark 5:25–34). It provoked me to taking communion sacraments privately at home.

There were times I wondered if the condition developed from the stress my body encountered from working with mental health consumers. Please do not take me the wrong way or put my thought out of context. I am admitting that it crossed my mind several times.

I am not saying that the mental health consumers caused the condition, but from a spiritual standpoint, mental illness is known as an unclean spirit or is interpreted as demonic. Mark 5:1–5 (KJV) comments:

> And they came over unto the other side of the sea, into the country of the Gadarenes. And when he was come out of the ship, immediately there met him out of the tombs a man with an unclean spirit, Who had his dwelling among the tombs; and no man could bind him, no, not with chains: Because that he had been often bound with fetters and chains, and the chains had been plucked asunder by him, and the fetters broken in pieces: neither could any man tame him. And always, night and day, he was in the mountains, and in the tombs, crying, and cutting himself with stones.

Now you see why the thought crossed my mind. Battling unusual spirits from the consumers I served at the prior employment was no joke. Those spirits were real and forceful and tried to latch on to me too! If you read further into the Gospel of Mark Chapter 5, there is a conversation between Jesus and the man with the unclean spirit.

> But when he saw Jesus afar off, he ran and worshipped him, And cried with a loud voice, and said, "What have I to do with thee, Jesus, thou Son of the most high God? I adjure thee by God, that thou torment me not." For he [Jesus] said unto him, "Come out of the man, thou unclean spirit." And he [Jesus] asked him, "What is thy name?" And he answered, saying, "My name is Legion: for we are many." (Mark 5:6–9, KJV)

Additionally, the Legion's or devil's requested to be transferred into a heard of pigs that were feeding near a sea. The Legions did not want to leave the country, and it was about two thousands of them! When Jesus cast the Legions out of the man, they entered into the pigs, and the pigs ran violently down into the sea and drown (Mark 5:6–13).

Another thought had me questioning if the attack on my body came from a few unclean spirits encountered at a church I once attended. I remember the spiritual service was high. I was near the altar where a few leaders of the church were standing. I felt consumed by the spirit of God, but suddenly, I felt something entered into me and went to the location of my uterine. It happened quickly, but I knew it was a serpent spirit that entered and attacked my uterus. Not only did I feel it, but also, it was as if I could see it in the spirit. I dropped to the floor and cried but continued to worship the Lord. Of course, I was puzzled and prayed to God about what happened to me near the altar that night at church. I kept reflecting on what I felt happened to me and what the unclean spirit looked like in which it was a serpent.

After seeking God about the unpleasant experience, I came across a small pamphlet that looked copied. On the front side, it had a picture of a cross that contained a circle and the backside, explained the original meaning about the particular cross, and specified the design found in Ireland and on the Isle of Iona. I opened the inside of the copied pamphlet and saw another cross, but it had a serpent wrapped around it; and immediately, the look of the serpent wrapped around the cross reminded me how I felt that night at the church service. The serpent wrapped on the cross inside the pamphlet is how it moved inside me. I got my answer. God verified my experience.

Although the serpent in the Bible has significant meaning in regards to Moses and the Israelites in the wilderness (Numbers 21:6–9), I could see a correlation of that biblical story and what happened to me that night at the altar. Most likely, one of the church leaders standing at the altar was apparently been jealous of the anointing on my life and knew my seed would be powerful. Through that person's jealousy, it sent the serpent spirit to inflict my reproductive organ.

But because I continued to worship the Lord, the serpent became a brass serpent that I looked upon and lived. As you keep reading, you will learn about the condition that I once had, which led me having to have surgery, and it will be clear to you about how I lived through the ordeal.

Lastly I do want you to know that I am knowledgeable that the condition I once had could be hereditary, and if the condition is looked at from a spiritual point of view, a generational curse is what it was.

> Keeping mercy for thousands, forgiving iniquity and transgressions and sin, and that will by no means clear the guilty; visiting the iniquity of the fathers upon the children, and upon the children's children, unto the third and to the fourth generation. (Exodus 34:7, KJV)

All right, with a deep sigh, I am ready to reveal the condition that robbed me from having children. I must discuss a few things first before revealing the ailment. I experienced a condition that started with me having issues with my menstrual cycle. I would have light to heavy cycles, and it would last during the normal cycle time (one week), and it would last three to four days sometimes (loved it when it lasts only for that length of time). I experienced severe menstrual cramping and spotting in between periods. Well, initially, fibrositis or fibromyalgia diagnosis was considered because I experienced a cyclic pattern of tender breasts and stomach bloating before my monthly cycle started.

The final diagnosis resulted in endometriosis due to me developing menstrual problems and my obstetric and gynecologist (ob-gyn) treated me several years for the diagnoses (fibrositis and endometriosis). Endometriosis was not what led me to having surgery. I will reveal it soon, but I have to let you know what I went through that led to another diagnosis, which lead to surgery. I had painful menstrual cycles, and when it was light bleeding (spotting two days), the bleeding looked pinkish in color. Then the spotting turned to heavy bleeding, and seemingly, the pain intensified. My ob-gyn treated me for this menstrual abnormality and tried two different types of birth control pills as part of the treatment regimen. One of the birth control pills supposedly caused my body to produce the estrogen it was lacking, and it worked for a while. I could see a change in my monthly cycle, and it appeared to be getting back to normal. But to make a long story short, the condition in my body worsened.

I started having cycles that went past one week. Sometimes, I bleed for two to three weeks. Most times, the bleeding started out heavy and lessened to a light bleeding and not stop until after two or three weeks. I can recall the bleeding started staying heavy and going past two to three weeks. Then my menstrual cycles got heavier and lasted for months. I bought a lot of black clothing (pants and skirts) for work. I figured that if I have an accident, the bleeding stains would not look obvious on black clothing. When working, I wore three sanitary pads for heavy menstrual flow along with several tissue paper around several sheets of paper towels that I folded to look like a pad. I would wrap the tissue paper around the sheets of paper towels. Eventually, from the heavy bleeding, I started passing clots of blood appearing dark red (almost black looking).

When at work, I would sit on the commode and let the clots pass. I could feel the clots when it was getting ready to pass, which was a good thing because most of the time, I could get to the bathroom before the clots passed. I constantly checked to see if I needed to change pads, the tissues, and sheets of paper towels. Most time, I only had to change the tissues and paper towels because the three thick pads held up well. Sometimes, I had to change the thick pads if a clot pass and I did not get to the bathroom in time. Whew, boy did not I worry and hoped that no blood got on my clothes. By this time, my ob-gyn had prescribed me ibuprofen eight hundred milligrams for pain. I remember while working that I would take half of the ibuprofen (four hundred milligrams), and it would last me the entire workday. As long as I moved around, the pain was tolerable. After work, I go home, elevate my feet, and take the other half of the ibuprofen. I would rest awhile while the ibuprofen kicked in. Then I get up and do whatever planned. And of course, I had to maintain wearing three thick pads, tissue, and several sheets of paper towels at home as well as at work and wherever I went.

I did not let the condition stop me from working or going on with life. I planned and developed a system that worked for me. In fact, I became creative in how to take an unpleasant situation and made it work for me! I do confess that there were times when the menstrual pain was severe, and I resulted to taking a whole eight hundred milligrams of ibuprofen, but I took it at home and not at work because not splitting the pill made me sleepy.

My system at work was taking a half ibuprofen during lunch and the other half around 4:00 p.m. I did not share with coworkers or other family members about the severity of the bleeding. My mother knew about the menstrual issues but no clue of how bad it was. I presented myself as masking what I was experiencing. I knew how much I could withstand and when to go home to rest and elevate my feet.

I maintained a level of motivation and continued to do the things that I enjoyed doing. The appointments with the ob-gyn became frequent for monitoring my hemoglobin, bleeding, and pain level. I lost weight and could wear a size 11 to 12 junior pants and jeans.

I discovered the size I could wear when I went to Walmart to purchase a few items. I stopped by the junior sizes and saw jeans that interested me. The jeans was a size 11 to 12, so I tried it on, and the fit was perfect. I could wear some of my other size pants because my stomach was bloating, and the bloating along with wearing a belt helped with keeping my pants on me. My mother immediately noticed that I was losing weight and told me, "You better start eating."

I would laugh it off and say, "I am eating."

The month of December had come, and the Christmas season was approaching. It is year 2004. My ob-gyn and I discussed about me having a hysterectomy. He expressed the hysterectomy was the solution due to my situation not improving but worsening. My hemoglobin had dropped as well as my weight, and the bleeding was not going to cease. I agreed to the surgery, which was to occur two days before Christmas. I revealed to my mother about the menstrual cycle problems, disclosed to her the frequent ob-gyn appointments, and surgery scheduled two days before Christmas. I did not feel peace about having the surgery. My thoughts were, *I could not have children, and there have to be other options for me.* I prayed to God about not having peace about the surgery. I believe he let me know not to have the surgery because the disturbance I felt in my spirit went away, so I called and cancelled the surgery that was one week prior to the scheduled surgery date.

Christmas passed, and the New Year 2005 came in. It was time to return to work because Christmas and New Year holiday were over. I am back at work going through the same motions and continuing carrying out my system developed regarding the eight-hundred-milligram ibuprofen. By now I am taking them a little too frequently and did not want to get addicted to them.

Now I am taking a half ibuprofen before going to work, lunchtime, and around 4:00 p.m. The pain was getting where it was becoming unbearable, and I would become teary-eyed sometimes on the job but could pull it together before anyone noticed. When I get home, I would take a whole ibuprofen and take another whole one before going to bed. I did not like what was happening with the eight-hundred-milligram ibuprofen and me. My body system is sensitive to medication, and I did not want to continue taking ibuprofen as I was doing.

Therefore, one morning during that workweek, I went to one of my coworkers' office who was an emergency services counselor and began to cry before letting her know what was wrong. The tears flowed, and I could not stop crying. When I tried to tell her what was wrong, I continued to cry. She kept asking me, "What's wrong, Phelia?"

Finally I pulled myself together and stopped crying. I shared with her about what was happening to me physically. I let her know everything on down to my creative homemade sanitary pads that I wear with the three sanitary pads for heavy flow to catch the heavy bleeding. I mentioned to her about the scheduled surgery during the Christmas break that did not occur and why I cancelled the surgery.

I mentioned having intense pain, passing heavy clots, and needing relief but do not know of a doctor who could help me. She grabbed my hands and said, "Let's pray and ask God for direction."

When we finished praying, she shared with me that our supervisor could help me. She informed our supervisor sees an ob-gyn doctor in Durham, North Carolina. I went to our supervisor disclosing to her about what was going on with me physically. She contacted her doctor's office on North Duke Street in Durham, North Carolina, and was able to get me an appointment the same month, if memory correct, but if not, it was not a long wait. I felt relieved and looked forward to going to the appointment. I thanked her more than once. She had nothing to say but good things about her doctor and felt the doctor that I would see for treatment would do a good job too. I could not see her doctor because he had no available opening to see me quickly.

The appointment day came, and I met the ob-gyn doctor who had been specializing in his practice his entire career. Everyone there was nice and helpful. My hemoglobin level continued to be low (level count: 6). My stomach, according to my ob-gyn doctor, looked like someone who was five months pregnant. I inquired about options to consider without having to have surgery. I expressed I have no children and that I like to have at least one. I finally got a diagnosis that fit my physical condition. The diagnosis was uterine fibroids. He explained that uterine fibroids are benign tumors, and fibroids could cause many symptoms depending on the size and with what was happening with me falls into the category.

My doctor and I discussed options from a pamphlet that he presented to me, which included several options to explore and he thoroughly explained each option. I ruled out one option known as uterine fibroid embolization, which is a procedure where a thin rod-like tube inserted into a blood vessel in the thigh area that will cut off blood flow to the fibroids by a substance injected through the rod-like tube. I remember thinking the procedure looked painful, and besides, it is a procedure for women who are not planning to have children in the future. At this particular appointment visit, my doctor prescribed iron pills to take three times a day to build my iron count.

I recollect the hysterectomy choice would be the last selection to consider. Another solution was Lupron injections which I consented to try. It was an expensive medication too! I tried it for three months and met with my ob-gyn monthly for monitoring. I recall while on the Lupron shot that the bleeding was not too bad the first month. In the second month, there was no bleeding. In the third month, the heavy bleeding started back but not immediately. I started back having a menstrual cycle with a normal flow, but it got heavier after five days and did not stop. My mother and I were at the mall in Martinsville, Liberty Fair mall but now it is a strip mall.

She noticed me walking funny as she described it, but I knew it was a shuffle gait. And she asked, "What is wrong with your legs?" My response was, "I don't know, but I need to sit down because I might fall."

I sat down for a few minutes. Then I stood up and told Momma I believe I can walk without any problems. She and I left the mall with me walking slowly and went home. I told her that at my next doctor's appointment, I would tell the doctor about what happened with my walking and would request to discontinue the Lupron injections. She agreed that I should not get Lupron shots anymore. By this time, Momma and a couple of others (coworkers) were suggesting what I should do about my situation. I decided to tune them out and tune out what I desired or thought was best for me and sought God for direction. After all, he knew what was best for me and the situation that I was facing.

One Saturday or may have been Sunday prior to my next doctor's appointment, my mother and I talked about the condition. She shared her experience from having a hysterectomy. Guess what, prior to my momma and I having the conversation, I came across a client who talked about she had a hysterectomy. Then at another occasion, there was a person talking about her hysterectomy experience, and neither the client nor that person knew I was at the crossroad of having to decide about having a hysterectomy. God was already directing me, but still I was not receptive.

The Saturday or Sunday that my mother and I discussed my medical issue, she pointed out I was losing weight and my face looking sunken. But I did not see my face as she described but did see my face as slimming down. I remember her asking me, "Pheia, do you want to live? If you do, you will have the surgery."

When she asked the question, it sounded like a loud bell ringing in my ears. My response was *yes*. I told her that when I go back for my doctor's appointment, I will tell him I want to have the hysterectomy surgery.

When I went back to my doctor's appointment, I told him about what happened to me at the mall. He replied never knowing Lupron causing people to walk with a shuffle gait. I said, "Maybe I am the first person to experience it from the med." He insisted that there was no research indicating it did. Our conversation went toward hysterectomy to stop the condition that had developed in me. I was hearing it and did not want to hear it. My iron count was still dropping, and I knew something had to occur soon. He gave me a pamphlet specifically on hysterectomy surgery. He discussed the surgery in detail. He explained why he would make a vertical incision instead of a horizontal incision below my belly button. He informed the size of the fibroid resulted in him having to perform the procedure the old way. He mentioned he will perform an appendectomy (remove my appendix) as I did not need it, and it would prevent having appendicitis later. He said that he would probably remove about five pounds of fat from my belly. I like hearing that the fat in my belly would be removed. My thought, *Wow, liposuction!* I told the doctor that I would have the hysterectomy surgery. I met with his staff who scheduled appointments, and after I finished with her and was immediately leaving her office, I felt like I could fly. The weight on me lifted. I did not realize that I was carrying around the heavy weight that I carried.

I got to a point in which I could not work eight hours a day. My ob-gyn had to reduce my workdays to half days. The reason for reducing me to half days had to do with low iron levels, and I stayed tired. Then it came to a point that I had to go out on medical leave. My doctor told me I would have a blood transfusion before the surgery. I did not want a blood transfusion and inquired about another alternative solution. My doctor continued the prescribed iron pills and put me on a beef diet that consisted of beef for breakfast, lunch, and dinner to build my iron level. By this point, the only thing that I had enough strength for is take a shower, put on pajamas, lay down, and watch TV.

Momma cooked me my favorite meat, which was beef cube steak smothered in gravy and onions. She fixed turnip greens and mashed potatoes, so dinner consisted of the beef cube steak and gravy with onions. Breakfast would be two boiled eggs, biscuit, and beef cube steak and gravy with onions. Of course, lunch was beef cube steak, gravy with onions, and bread. Did I ever get tired of eating it? No, I did not. My momma could fix the best beef cube steak smothered in onions and gravy in the entire wide world. My mother made homemade gravy. It was not gravy from the can or a jar. The closest to my mother's beef cube steak and gravy is K&W restaurant, so now when I get a taste for it, I go to the K&W in Roanoke, Virginia, or Greensboro, North Carolina. Beef cube steak was my diet plan until I had the surgery.

It was June 2005, and I had another scheduled doctor's appointment a week prior before the surgery to see if my iron level increased or not. My iron level was 11, which was good. I continued the iron pills as prescribed and the beef diet. The surgery went as scheduled the following Monday.

It is now Monday morning around 6:00 a.m. My mother, maternal aunt, and first cousin on my father's side of the family who is a registered nurse and I were in Durham, North Carolina, at the hospital. The hospital nurse prepped me for surgery, and I did not know that shaving the most private area of my body, which identifies my womanhood, would occur. Some kind of way I was not informed that shaving would happen or did not think to ask when I was told by my doctor that he would do a vertical cut from my navel toward the vaginal area. I felt stripped and shamed! Before the nurse left, she told me an anesthesiologist would come to see me shortly to start the medicine that will put me under for the duration of the surgery.

When the nurse left, I told my cousin that I did not know my private area would be shaved. She said, "Yeah," while looking upward as if she was looking at something over my head to avoid eye contact, and the look indicated it would be all right. I reminded her about the Scripture to read me before I am wheeled in for surgery. I told her that I did not want my mother to see me cry. My cousin laughed and said, "Your momma told me she did not want you to see her cry."

My cousin read the Scripture that I requested, but for some unusual reason, I cannot remember the Scripture. All I recount is that it came from the book of Psalm, but which Psalm? I do not know! How frustrating it is for me not to remember. Oh, well, I shall keep my story moving. The anesthesiologist came in and did what he is trained to do, and while the medicine was going in, I began to shake. I expressed feeling cold, and he added Ativan medicine to control the shaking. It worked too! I looked at my mother, aunt, and cousin and smiled. And off to the operating room I went.

In the operating room, I could see the doctor scrubbing his arms from the elbow down to his hands. The nurse talk to me about what was going to happen, and the next thing I knew, I looked up at the bright lights hanging from the ceiling and thinking, *God, I trust you*, and feeling at peace, I went out like a blown light bulb. Did I mention before ever thinking about surgery? I dreamed being in an operating room looking at bright lights. Of course, when they lifted me from the hospital bed onto the operating room table, while lying on my back, I saw the bright lights and experienced a flashback about the dream. God had prepared me and really, I did not recognize it at the time. He had already presented me with the solution for the physical problem, but his answer was not what I wanted. Since his resolution was not my choice, I could not see it. I was rejecting his plan for my life.

> For my thoughts are not your thoughts, neither are your ways my ways, saith the LORD. For as the heavens are higher than the earth, so are my ways higher than your ways, and my thoughts than your thoughts. (Isaiah 56:8–9, KJV).

He has a bigger plan, and even when I could not see it, all was working together for my good. When the surgery was over, a nurse hovered over me saying, "Miss Griggs, Miss Griggs." I slowly opened my eyes, and she said, "You are in the recovery room."

I could hear another patient, a male patient, telling a nurse that he wanted to go home to his wife. The nurse told him, "You would see your wife shortly. She is in the waiting room." The man tried to get out the bed, and how did I know this? The nurse said, "Mister so and so, you cannot get out the bed." By then, I was feeling annoyed and told the nurse, "I wish that man would be quiet." The nurse mentioned many times after men have surgery they think they can go straight home. I made an ump sound and closed my eyes to signal I want to rest.

Finally I am out of the recovery room and was put in a private room on the floor that they put women who have had a baby. My legs were encased inside stockings that where attached to a machine that massage them whenever I turn them. My hospital bed was a special bed. It massaged my body. I was treated with special care and was appreciative. The hospital staff made sure that I would not form any blood clots. When my mother, aunt, and cousin came in my room, the first thing I requested was to see a mirror. They looked at one another in agreement without saying the word *no*. I requested again to see a mirror, not caring about what they thought I did not need to see. I won, and the next thing I knew, I had a mirror in my hand. I took one look and said okay and gave the mirror to my aunt. My face looked pale, almost white as the stockings on my legs and the blanket and sheet covering me. I said to them, "I just wanted to see what I look like."

I wanted to know everything they did while I was in surgery. I asked, "Where did you all go eat?" They said they found a restaurant near the hospital and ate there. They told me that I was in surgery longer than expected. The doctor had a slight complication. The doctor told my momma, aunt, and cousin (according to them) that the fibroids where not only attached to the outside of my womb but had formed on the inside of my womb and got in position to pass out of me like a child coming forth through the birth canal.

My mom said, "If that had happened to you, you probably would lost your mind seeing something like that in the floor." They mentioned the doctor said the fibroids were the length of a pencil. I was so glad to see my family. I guess when they saw that I was not moved by how I look when I looked in the mirror, they felt revealing everything to me about what the doctor told them would be okay. Truthfully, they were correct because I wanted to know everything.

Before my mother, aunt, and cousin left to return to Martinsville, Virginia, the nurse came in letting me know how to move around and that my stay in the hospital should be three days. She let me know I could push the button to get more pain medicine (morphine) when feeling like I needed it. I was hungry and wanted food but could only have a liquid diet until the next day, so I had to settle for the liquids as if I could have it my way. Who was I kidding? No one but myself. We (my mother, aunt, cousin, and I) thank God for bringing me through the surgery. They gave me a hug and left, saying, "I will call you tomorrow." I was a big girl but Momma's little girl. However, she saw that I would be fine and could walk away in peace.

Now I am in my hospital room and feeling pain. I pushed the button to get pain medicine and drifted off to sleep. In the midst of sleeping, I thought I was falling out of the bed. When I came to, I pushed the call bell for the nurse. She came to see what I wanted, and I told her I felt like I was falling out of the bed. She smiled and said, "You cannot fall out of the bed. That is why the rails are up on each side of the bed. We know the pain medicine has the tendency to make patients think they are falling." She asked, "Do you need to go to the bathroom?"

I responded, "I might as well because I need to move around to get the soreness out." I was sore but was determined not to be defeated.

My doctor checked in on me the next day to see how I was managing. He talked with me about those fibroids he removed. He showed me a picture of one of the fibroids. It was next to a pencil to show its length. He explained my case, being a rare case, is a good tool for educational purpose. He asked if Duke School of Medicine could use the fibroids removed from me for educational purposes. I gave my blessing by signing papers, allowing them to use my fibroids for their scientific research and any other methods to benefit science and people (at least that is how I saw it). I let my doctor know there was slight swelling on the left side of my belly, but the right side was flat. He looked sort of concerned, but then maybe that is what I read into it. He assured me that the swelling would go down and that I would be fine.

The next day, an intern followed up on my care, and wow, did not he look fine! I was washing up in the bathroom and thought, *I would not care if he saw me naked!* Although I confessed I felt shy, I played it off, and seemingly the smile on my face stretched to the hospital parking lot. I told him to let me cover up, and we can talk. I really do not know if I heard anything he said because I was mesmerized by how handsome he looked. He had dark hair, brown eyes, nice built, and right height. He was not a sore eye but pleasant to behold! His doctor's uniform crispy white with his name in blue writing fits who he was and what he was about, and that was helping someone like me (laughing). He asked the basic questions and wanted to know if I had any concerns, which I did not. He told me to continue what I was doing to get better to return home. I did not see him anymore after that day, but I got a boost to keep doing my routine walk and work on passing gas so that I could go home.

During the first night stay in the hospital, my moving around was from the bed to the bathroom. On the second day when I could eat, each time I had to go to the bathroom, I would walk to the nursing station and circle the hall that goes back to the location of my room. If I were up at 2:00 a.m. using the bathroom, I would do my routine walk to the nursing station and circle the hall that goes back to the location of my room. I will let you in on a secret, I was nosey and acted as if I did not pay any attention to what the nurses where discussing. Trust me, I could not tell you what they talked about because I do not remember. Apparently, it was not anything juicy because if it were, I would remember. Still trying to pass gas and praying, "Lord, let me pass gas, so I can go home. Don't wanna be in this hospital five days," and I laughed at myself.

Now it is day three. No gas passed yet! I am still doing my routine walk and feeling better too. I ate breakfast and decided that I would walk before washing up. I recall seeing in my distance a colorful top on this young black woman. I thought *a coat of many colors* is what her top reminds me.

"You know, the biblical story of Joseph and his father Israel." Israel favored Joseph over his other sons and the coat exemplified his love (Genesis 37:3–4). The colors of the woman's top fashioned my eyes to it and upon almost, passing her in the hall, I complimented her about her top. She smiled, and our conversation started. She asked, "Is your baby a boy or girl?" Remember, I mentioned after surgery that I was wheel to the baby ward for care.

I responded, "No, no child...had a partial hysterectomy. I did get to keep my ovaries. Maybe in the future, I could do one of those surrogate births," and I smiled. She said, "I am sorry...you know, the doctor is saying I need to have a hysterectomy too." That was my conversation with the woman who had on a top of many colors. I expressed how sorry that I am for her. Then I said, "Do you have children?"

She responded, "Yes, I have one child but would like to have another child. And that is why I am not sure about having a hysterectomy." She proceeded to share, "My husband and I would like another child. What was happening to you that led to your surgery?"

I explained to her about all that I had endured and that, finally, it came to a point that a *challenging decision* had to occur. I suggested to her to get somewhere quiet, tune out everyone's suggestions, including her own, and see what God has to say. I told her he would not lead her wrong. He knows our today, tomorrow, and future; so be receptive to his leading.

She thanked me and said, "Sounds like a good idea. Had not thought about getting somewhere quiet and allow God to direct me." We said our goodbyes, and she walked off. I walked back to my room and thought, *That is why I was attracted to her top. God ordained our paths to cross.*

The woman and I had commonality. She was concerned about what to do and knew she needed to make a decision soon. As I was in the beginning, I did not want a hysterectomy and neither did she. We both were concerned about having a child and knew the hysterectomy would hinder our desire.

Guess what! I finally passed gas that night. I was so excited, grinning from ear to ear, and could not wait to tell the nurse. I went to the nursing station feeling all chirpy internally. And when I revealed "I passed gas," the nurse looked at me with no expression. And the other nurses in the area had no comment. They continued to do what they were doing. I am thinking, *Say something. Show me some sort of emotion and don't just look stoned!*

Then I blurted out, "I was told to let you all know when I pass gas." The nurse said *okay* and continued to do what she was doing. I left the nursing station to go back to my room feeling as if my balloon of happiness was stuck with a pin. Of course, I processed and processed what had just happened to me at the nursing station. I believe my feelings crushed, and quickly, I realized it was not about me. I told myself, "There are other people on this floor needing care too."

Day four and it is discharge time, and happy am I! Momma and auntie were working, so an ex coworker who attended the same church as I transported me home from the hospital. Boy, when I stepped outside on the sunny day, the air felt fresh and new. I was beyond grateful to be alive! I tell you that having major surgery and before going into the surgery, I knew the result could be death, but God, who is rich in grace and mercy, saw fit to let me live. Hallelujah! The surgery left me with a scar from below my navel downward, but to me, it is a beauty mark that reminds me of what my God can do. There are creams such as Mederma that would take away the scar, but I chose not to use it. The scar is my permanent tattoo in remembrance of what Jesus did for me.

There were adjustments done to make reaching dishes and anything needed in the cabinets easier to grab. I could not mop or sweep the floors. Thank God for Momma (I miss her so). My momma did light cleaning for me until I was able to do it myself. I could not drive for eight weeks and stayed out of work for eight weeks. I considered myself smart and did not rush to return to work because to be in full strength was my desire. I love wearing high heel shoes and could not wear them. I prayed, "Lord, please don't take my high heels away from me."

Eventually, I did return to wearing high heels, but now, I only wear two or two-and-half inch heels. For several months when I went to get groceries, I requested the bagboy to put my groceries in the trunk of my car. When I got home, I would look for my neighbor to bring the heavy items in the house such as twenty-four count of bottled water. I became smart by splitting my groceries, meaning not buy a lot at one time. How well do I remember thinking, *Was I ready to clean my bathtub?* I kneeled down to clean the bathtub, and something pulled my insides right at my navel, and it pained! It was a sharp, dull pain, and you know it took a whole year before I fully recovered from the hysterectomy surgery.

I always heard that you would dream about your menstrual cycle once it is gone but thought it was a myth. I found out it was not a myth because it happened to me. I dreamt my cycle was on, and when I woke up from the dream, I was overjoyed that I had no more cycles. Wow! No more buying sanitary pads, cramping, bloating, and mood swings! If I chose, I could wear light color pants, skirts, and dresses. I was free, and it felt good! Monthly, for a while, I could smell blood and would have tender breasts. It was one of those things that my body had to adjust regarding no longer having a womb; it cannot produce menstrual flows anymore. Good written, goodbye, audios, sayonara, and so long because you are not welcome here anymore! What a relief! No more homemade pads to catch the heavy flow! No more worrying if I would have an accident on my clothes! "Who are you kidding? Not me. I'm done and glad about it!"

As a child, I remember hearing grown folks talk about knowing "so and so had a hysterectomy and lost her mind." Not having a womb did not bother me nor does it bother me now. I see the good in the entire situation; and that is, at least, I have my ovaries. I have a sound mind and feel good about me as a woman, and my womanhood is not depleted (smile). Life dealt me a challenging situation that went south and beyond my control. I faced a *challenging decision* to have the major surgery to correct a female problem that was getting out of control. After kicking and screaming (exaggerating) about what I thought would be best for me, I took charge of what *was* best for me with God's help. I do not remember crying because of having to give up my womb; I remember viewing it as a total relief. I saw my life as not interrupted by heavy bleeding and clots flowing from me. I saw my life as now I can go places and not wonder if blood would appear on my clothes.

Well, my faith in God's judgment and standing on the Scripture, Isaiah 54:1, has been my consolation.

> "Sing, O barren, thou that didst not bear; break forth into singing, and cry aloud, thou that didst not travail with child: for more are the children of the desolate than the children of the married wife," saith the Lord. (Isaiah 54:1, KJV)

Believe me, I have had more than one talk with God about why my lot in life is not to have a child or experience childbirth. The result of those conversations bring peace and acceptance every time. If I bring it up to him now in a mental flash, I do not need an answer but only to let him know that I know he has not forgotten me, will always be there for me, and will make it up to me.

# CHAPTER 12

# *Life*

Sometimes, we do not understand the will of God for our lives, and I am not saying that not able to bare children was God doing because it was not. His will is perfect with order and structure. He created woman and man and blessed them saying, "Be fruitful and multiply" (have children) (Genesis 1:28). My perspective is that the fall of man (Adam) is the root to injustices that occur in *life*. Adam and Eve were conned by a crafty con artist, the serpent, which lead to the punishment of damnation. They became a prey to the serpent and a bait!

However, the beauty of it all is that we can have redemption through Jesus Christ, which is a choice. You can chose Christ and live or settle for less and serve Satan himself. God is a gentleman and does not force himself on anyone. He left the choice up to us, so I encourage you to choose *life* and live. As a result, when this *life* is over, there is a home not made by hands but a home in the heavens where there is no trouble, crying, dying, starvation, sexual assault, and sexual harassment. There is no murdering, backbiting, lying, cheating, misery, and pain. There is no depression and oppression. There is no earthly disasters and any manner of evil happenings, which occur in our world today.

For John, in the book of Revelation reveals what he saw while on the isle of Patmos while in the Spirit on the Lord's Day (Revelation 1:9–10). John, in Revelation 21:1–5 (KJV), said:

And I saw a new heaven and a new earth: for the first heaven and the first earth were passed away; and there was no more sea. And I John saw the holy city, new Jerusalem, coming down from God out of heaven, prepare as a bride adorned for her husband.

And I heard a great voice out of heaven saying, "Behold, the tabernacle of God is with men, and he will dwell with them, and they shall be his people, and God himself shall be with them, and be their God. And God shall wipe away all tears from their eyes; and there shall be no more death, neither sorrow, nor crying, neither shall there be any more pain: for the former things are passed away [former things are the previous earthly occurrences; earth itself]."

And he that sat upon the throne said, "Behold, I make all things new." And he said unto me, "Write: for these words are true and faithful."

Understanding the causes and effects of *life* help with coping with situations that are beyond me. Yes, I have often wondered what my seed (child) would look like if I had one. What personality would he or she possess? He or she would be of what skin tone? Would he or she make an impact on the world? Would he or she be like me, desire to help others, and help others to see their potential, so they can go forth in *life* and mark territories?

Being childless has its pros and cons. From the pros side, I do not have to witness burying my child or my child witness burying me. I do not have to worry about my child's safety or the overall burden of parenthood. The cons side of not having a child is having him or her in my *life* to love and nurture, to correct and say, "I am the momma. When you get a job and move out of the home, then you can do as you please. But while you are under my roof, you do as

I say do." Wow, the joys of parenthood was not my life's path; but at times, I extend a motherly love to other peoples' children.

It is amusing whenever I am in a store and a mother's child acts out. The mother seemed like she cannot do anything with her child, or maybe she is tired because she is a single parent. Possibly, she is not a single parent but a married parent who feels she is raising the child with little to no support from her spouse. Shoot, I do not know what the reasons could be! Well, getting back to the child acting out, I would make eye contact with the child giving him or her the *eye* like my mother used to do to me, and the child would stop crying or do what his or her mother told him or her.

One time in a clothing store, I gave a child (female) the *eye*, and the child clutch ahold to her mother's pants leg while looking back at me as if she was afraid that I would whoop her. I smiled and laughed all at the same time. The child was going in and out of the clothes hanging on the clothes rack, and her mother told her to stop. When she came from underneath the clothes, I gave her the *eye*! She was a smart little something, too! When she figured out that I was not going to whoop her, she went back to doing the same thing—going in and out of the clothes on the clothes rack—but little did she know what her momma would do next. Her mother smacked her bottom, and I looked at her as if to say, "I told you so." I felt compassion and looked at the child with an awl look, and she quickly turned her head in another direction, sniffling. I continued to shop and found a few nice items from that clothing rack.

My challenging decision revealed in Chapter 11. It challenged me and added courage and growth. I learned a little bit more about myself and what I could do. I took on a new attitude about how I perceived things in life that occurred not as I would want them. My relationship with Christ grew as well. My faith in God came alive regarding accepting not having a child and not charging him as doing this to me. My faith in God believes that he has my life in his hands and directs it accordingly. When I elected to allow him to be my Lord and Savior Jesus Christ, I gave up what I want in life to have what he sees best for me in life. I acknowledge that not always do I want to go his route and had times when I was frustrated and felt rejected. I would say to God, "I feel like you are hiding me or what will become of my life." I had my battles with God many times. But each time, he always win, and I would decipher his way is the better way.

I sure am glad that I finally stopped fighting with God and more receptive to his will for my life. Taking care of my mother when she became terminally ill put me in the position to grow up. Now do not twist it. It was not as if I could not think for myself or make a life for myself. I had to let go of being spoiled. You know, no longer it being I getting the attention or seeing things my way or it is me and about what I want.

Me, myself, and I started shedding little by little. I realized too that the path I was on goes to a level in which God has my feet in a spacious place. I will come out of this path with new insight, vision, and dedication. I would see the true meaning of family and how important family is. I discovered that family does not take a back seat when it comes to doing things for the community or what we may see as kingdom work.

How did I come to this knowledge? Well, my mother needed me. She had a desire, and that was not to let her die in a nursing home. She was a divorcee. I was all she had besides her sister and brother (living at the time), but a daughter-and-mother relationship is not the same as sibling relationship. There came a time when I wanted to attend church while my mom needed me home with her, and what God showed me is that I wanted to escape from my responsibilities as a daughter to my mother. I wanted to run from the situation that life brought about. I had rather remained complacent to what I had come accustomed to doing in life and avoided dealing with challenges. All along, God was saying, "I would take the unfortunate situation and grow you for my purpose." Even now I see life entirely different.

Do not misconstrue that doing kingdom work should continue when a loved one needs you. The question is, do others understand? God understands and knows that your work in the kingdom will not suffer if you have to halt and put attention in a needed direction that will take from others who have grown accustomed to you always being at their beckon call. Paul implies in 1Corinthians 3:6–7 (KJV), "I have planted, Apollos watered; but God gave the increase. So then neither is he that planted anything, neither he that watereth; but God that giveth the increase."

See? What we do in the kingdom for God is his multiplication. We are a vessel used by God to do the planting, but he takes it from there and increased what you may have planted and what I may have watered. Understand that not you nor I can get the credit.

Therefore, when a loved one needs you—whether the person is ill or have a ball game, recital, or concert—incline to that person's need. Did not God institute family? Shall our family go lacking when in need whether spiritual, physical, mental, or all three? Sometimes, the sacrifice just may be for a friend, coworker, or stranger.

I believe God does not see our work in the vineyard (ministry) as man does, but we can see how he views it if we seek his face. He will let us know if we are off base with our perceptions about others who, momentarily, take a break from working in the vineyard due to various reasons that led to that decision. The importance about a sabbatical from working in the vineyard is that you and God know why and you have peace about it. Besides, it does not mean that you have taken a break from God or ministering responsibilities (serving).

I mentioned that I see life differently now, and this is what I mean. When it is all over, meaning when life ends, all earthly possessions would stay behind. What is most important is what legacy you would leave behind. How would this generation remember you? What would you leave that is beneficial to your family, church family, community, and society? The Word of God lets us know that it is appointed once for man to die then the judgment (Hebrews 9:27).

Humanity cannot get around this truth. Man, woman, boy, girl, old, or young have to travel this path. In the book of Job, Job points out, "Naked came I out of my mother's womb, and naked shall I return thither: the LORD gave, and the LORD hath taken away; blessed be the name of the LORD" (Job1:21, KJV).

Job understood that man's days upon the earth is just a breath. He understood he brought nothing into this world and will exit it with nothing.

I faced a challenging decision to have major surgery or not. And if not, I would eventually put myself in harm's way. In addition, having the surgery and not knowing if I would survive put me in harm's way. Either way, I had to make a decision. I specify this to indicate that you too will have a *challenging decision* to make about where to spend eternity. I was able to make a decision God already had planned for me, but if I had not included him in my decision, the result may have been another way. You may think to yourself and feel, possibly, that time was not on my side. Well, think again, time is never on anyone side. God is time, and our times are in his hands (Psalm 39:5 and Psalm 31:15). Give him your life today and start bonding with him.

Let not Satan steal what Christ has rightfully purchased. He purchased you and me when he became the second Adam to die for us because he was without sin and God, his Father, loved us so much that he gave his only Son for ransom to unite us back unto him.

In the book of John, it is mentioned about how much the Father loves us by signifying this, "For God so loved the world, that he gave his only begotten Son, that whosoever believeth in him should not perish, but have everlasting life" (John 3:16, KJV). Chose Christ today and live! Christ *is* coming back to gather his church, so why not open your heart and let the church start in you? Amen.

# *Appendix Poem*

## Life Is

Life is starting out as an infant,
growing into a man or woman,
reproducing a child one after another,
and sharing the love for your sister and brother.

Life is having fun in your teenage days,
no worries until you are out on your way,
experiencing the goodness and hardness—
that comes naturally day to day.

Life is reaching the old age—
where you surrender to everything,
taking the time out to spend the wonderfulness
and joyfulness of your grandchildren,
knowing that there is generation after generation—
until the world may end someday.

Life is sharing the tears of living and dying,
knowing that there's end of breathing—
Whether ending at birth, old or young.

My maternal grandfather, George Washington Griggs, passed while I was an eighth grader, which inspired me to write the poem "Life Is."

The poem is on page 15 in the Tapestry section of my 1981 Volume 7 Fieldale-Collinsville High School annual.

The poem's original format was revised in 2018 by the author. There are no word changes from the original poem.

# About the Author

Dr. Ophelia Griggs is a native of Martinsville and Henry County. She attended Henry County Public Schools. She received her bachelor's degree from Norfolk State University in Sociology 1986, a master's degree in Community and College Counseling from Longwood University in 2004, and a doctorate degree in Education with a specialization in leadership and management from Capella University in August 2016.

Dr. Griggs obtained a career studies certificate in community services leadership from Patrick Henry Community College in 2008. She has theological studies through Jacksonville Theological Seminary mid-1990s.

Dr. Griggs has worked several human services jobs. Currently, she works at Patrick Henry Community College in Student Support Services. Dr. Griggs is an active member of Virginia Organizing nonprofit grassroots organization. Through this organization, she has learned to be a voice for her community and a voice on a statewide level. In 2013, Dr. Griggs, along with 135 Virginia Organizing representatives of Virginia, attended a White House meeting.

Dr. Griggs is an ordained and licensed minister and serves as an associate minister at Refuge Temple Ministries under the leadership of Elder Alan Preston in Martinsville, Virginia. She served as a volunteer chaplain for Memorial Hospital of Martinsville and Henry County now known as SOVAH Health Martinsville.

Recently, she started blogging about mental health, hoping those needing mental health care would not hide it but get help. She looks forward to her first published book, a memoir about supernatural experiences, her family, herself, and religious views.

Dr. Griggs credits every accomplishment and the ones to come to Almighty God and knows it is because of him that she lives, moves, and has her being.